The Fearless Executive

The High Performers Guide to Managing Your Thoughts, Controlling Your Emotions & Implementing Life Changing Actions

BY

KRISTINA MADDEN

THE FEARLESS EXECUTIVE

Ordering Information: Quantity sales. Special discounts are available on quantity purchases by corporations, associations, and others. Orders by U.S. trade bookstores and wholesalers.

DREAMSTARTERS

www.DreamStartersPublishing.com

Table of Contents

Dedication

First and foremost, I want to thank God.

My endless journey of growing closer to God is the reason I can write this book and have an impact on people. He has called me, molded and shaped me into the person I am today. The Fearless Executive.

I am dedicating this book to my grandfather, "papaw", the man. Jim Mullins Sr. A retired chief master sgt, a leader, teacher, and someone that truly loves people. This is a man that would never miss a phone call and greet you with excitement and eagerness to have a conversation and talk about the world, life and everything in between. A man filled with wisdom. In recent months he lost a battle with cancer, and I got to spend countless precious hours and days by his side during the unexpectedly fast process. I learned about his faith on a new level. My faith grew. I learned about impact, leadership, and what a true positive attitude looks like. It made me realize my longing for more out of life and my desire to impact people comes from somewhere in my bloodline.

The most exciting part…I got to show him this book in full print before his last days on earth. And I swear, no one has ever lit up about my achievements in quite the way he did, and I'm not sure anyone ever will. A moment forever in my memory. There is something sacred shared between a grandfather and granddaughter. I am so honored and blessed to have had him in my life for the time that I did. I know he's reading it under the warm glow of a sunny day in a better place.

Next, my son, he is our true WHY! He inspires me daily as he pushes through the challenges of autism. He is committed to step into his gifts and pursue his goals daily. He is the happiest, most free-spirited person I know, and I push to grow and build our life and business because of him! He is a fearless executive in the making.

My husband, Tim Madden, I may not want to admit it, but he makes it ALL happen in our life. He said he knew I was the one on our first date. Every dream we set out to run toward, he has seen them to the finish line! He is the steadfast support my son and I have grown to rely on. Day in and day out he shows me what TRUE unconditional love is. He is an example of what discipline looks like. He meets me where I am and continues to say YES to all my crazy ideas…like writing this book. He made best seller before me! Thank you LOVE!! You amaze me every day!

Last but definitely not least, my family, friends and the team at Executive Career Upgrades. Without the inner workings of these relationships and support, none of this would be possible! When I wake up, I know I can reach out to people near and far that have full belief in me, my mission and have love and support to offer! Our staff is endlessly brought into the mission and Tim, and I are so blessed that we can place this company so dear to our hearts in the hands of leaders in our organization that are willing to see it through.

Special shout out to Maigan Willard, my Executive Assistant, she is an extension of me and helps our vision come to life every day! She also pushed me to slow down, reflect and enjoy the process of writing this dedication page. I'm so glad she did!

The Executive Career Upgrades clients for pushing themselves, for trusting me with their career and path to a better mindset and life. I wouldn't be #CoachKristinaMadden without you. My hope is that you always find your way back to the truth-that you are capable and worthy of all your dreams. When the odds seem stacked against you and the lies are loud, I hope what you have learned here with us has positioned you to claw your way out of hopelessness and back into a world of limitless possibilities. I believe everything is in your favor. You are the leaders of the world. You are the real fearless executives.

The Mission Statement

To help ambitious business executives reach their full professional and personal potential, we at Executive Career Upgrades are committed to training, motivating, and directing them toward that end.

We encourage the development of corporate leaders in an environment that facilitates career advancement through cooperation, technology, and pushing for peak performance.

In a world that is recovering from the epidemic, Executive Career Upgrades is the place where the expansion of businesses becomes feasible. We are the globe of business's last best chance.

Introduction

Do you ever find yourself at a crossroads in your career and at a loss for what to do next? Do you feel like you can't achieve your goals because of uncertainty and fear? Most of us can relate to these sentiments at some point in our lives. It's a common aspiration to have a successful and rewarding career, but fear often stands in the way.

Welcome to a book committed to helping you conquer your fears. This book will enable you to move toward your ideal career. It will give you the tools you need to overcome obstacles in your professional life and take the next step toward realizing your full potential.

Fear of being rejected, fear of failing, and fear of uncertainty can keep us from taking risks. Those risks are necessary to find employment that truly fulfills us. Fear can also keep us from finding work that sparks any interest at all. Sometimes we doubt our abilities and worry that we don't have what it takes to be successful.

But what if I assured you that dread doesn't have to prevent you from moving forward? What if you were to transform your fears into motivation to drive you forward toward fulfillment and success?

THE FEARLESS EXECUTIVE

The knowledge I will share in this book comes from my own firsthand experiences. I don't consider myself a "guru" or "motivational speaker" who's never experienced doubt or uncertainty in my life. I can relate to where you are because I have been there myself. I know what it's like to be paralyzed by doubt and anxiety as you attempt to chart your professional course.

I've often questioned my worth and suffered from impostor syndrome. These fears undoubtedly made it hard for me to take chances and follow my passions. I've also had my share of setbacks and disapproval along the road. But I've realized I can overcome my fears and move forward despite everything that's happened to me.

When channeled properly, fear can transform into a potent motivator that drives us toward success. Humans have an innate response to danger that serves as a vital protection mechanism. It allows us to spot dangers and take preventative measures. Fear, however, can be a detriment if it keeps us from taking steps toward our objectives.

For example, we might not attempt new things, pass up on opportunities, or resist trying anything new if we fear failing. However, "positive thinking" and "mindset shifts" are not the only topics covered in this book. I understand that fear is a multifaceted emotion that cannot be overcome quickly. That's why I've sprinkled the book with actions and suggestions designed to get you not only thinking critically about your fears but also taking concrete steps toward overcoming them.

This book is about the origins of fear and the ways it shows up in people's lives. We'll discuss the various forms of fear and how they influence our thought processes. We'll also discuss why they're so hard to get past. I'll give you some tried-and-true methods for facing your fears and getting the ball rolling on your dreams. Learn how to use these methods to foster a growth mentality through concrete examples from my own life.

Along the way, I'll share advice on how to remain motivated despite setbacks that are inevitable in any career. You'll hear inspiring true accounts of people who overcame tremendous odds to achieve remarkable success. Reading these accounts will help you realize that you are not alone.

These anecdotes serve as catalysts for you to find your purpose and pursue it. I wrote this book to help you overcome your fears and realize your full potential. I want to show you how to overcome obstacles and use your anxiety to drive you forward. There's a chance this book can change your life for the better, but it will require time and effort. That's why I peppered this book with thought-provoking questions and actions designed to help you examine your fears. This will help you find productive solutions to them.

Taking steps toward your objectives, no matter how far out of your comfort zone they may be, is the ultimate key to overcoming fear. I'm writing this book to give you the drive, enthusiasm, and valuable advice you need to achieve your goals.

I'm not promising you'll be successful immediately, nor can I give you a foolproof way to face your fears. But I can say with confidence that if you put in the effort, you will find this book to be an invaluable resource that will help you realize your full potential. This knowledge will launch you toward the dream professional life you've always imagined.

When you face your fears head-on, you can use them as motivation to push yourself to new heights. Are you ready to do just that? Then let's dive right in!

Chapter 1

Fear, Freedom, Facts, Feelings

"The phrase "do not be afraid" is written in the Bible 365 times. That's a daily reminder from God to live every day fearlessly."

Anonymous

We experience a wide range of feelings in reaction to the almost daily exposure we have to tragedy, trauma, and injustice. When we're feeling anxious or angry, we may try to find comfort from external sources. Being fearless is challenging, especially when our external world is constantly shifting.

The mental and physical toll of constantly being on edge is immense. The emotional strain of fear can cloud our judgment and cause us to act irrationally. When we're anxious, our concentration tends to narrow as we look for anything that might pose a threat. Fear impairs our ability to evaluate situations rationally and take appropriate action.

This is a call to stop letting your fears rule your life. By ditching our fears, we can make the world a better place.

The Four Fs—fear, freedom, facts, and feelings—are a robust basis for personal development and change. One way to overcome self-limiting beliefs is to distinguish between facts and feelings. We must start using fear as a driving force rather than letting it hold us back. Let me take you on a journey of self-improvement as we delve into the Four Fs and find your full potential.

Driving Life by Emotions

"Researchers have found that even more than IQ, your emotional awareness and abilities to handle feelings will determine your success and happiness in all walks of life, including family relationships" (Pilon, 2019)

John Gottman

Acknowledging our feelings is important because they tell us something useful about ourselves. They can help us grow as individuals. To move past certain wounds, it's necessary to feel them and let them go. On the other hand, letting emotions determine your actions rather than rational thought can be disastrous. When we allow our feelings to dominate our decisions and behavior, problems arise.

Let's compare it to driving a car. Your identity is intertwined with your car. When you're behind the wheel, you're in charge of where the car goes, how fast it goes, and whether it crashes. Imagine everything is going swimmingly. The sun is out, there's no traffic, the roads are in excellent condition, and everyone seems happy.

Then suddenly you run into roadblocks. These roadblocks are allegories of everyday difficulties. A flat tire could represent a health problem. Stormy weather could indicate a family issue. A traffic jam can mean loss of employment, and a massive accident may be a detour such as the end of a relationship.

All these life-altering events give rise to a wide range of emotions. You might experience rage, fear, frustration, sorrow, grief, or anxiety. Having control of your life while dealing with the wide range of feelings you're bound to experience is a struggle.

When you let these feelings take the wheel, you give up all responsibility for the vehicle's course, pace, and security. You could drive off bridges, into gullies, or oncoming traffic. Your emotional state determines your decisions and behaviors, which can have negative consequences.

Those emotions have zero driving skills! It's like trusting a kid who can't reach the pedals, can't see the road, and can't read with the wheel of a car while you sleep in the backseat. Instead, don't give in to your feelings. Stop the car and invite them to sit anywhere behind the driver, including the front passenger. Recognize them and allow them to ride along, but never let them drive.

After you hear, understand, and value these feelings, they can safely exit the car. While they may temporarily change the course of your life, you are responsible for the decisions you make and the path you choose to take, so always put yourself in the driver's seat.

Being Spun Out by Emotions

A great mentor of mine shared a powerful thought that has been a navigating tool for me ever since.

In his words,

"High emotions can equal low intelligence."

Mentor Brandon Dawson

KRISTINA MADDEN

My feelings were once my biggest obstacles. I used to work for Chanel selling high-end cosmetics. Whenever I made a mistake—real or imagined—I would immediately sink into a deep well of self-doubt and hatred. It was as if I was stuck in an endless loop of despair from which there was no way out.

The worst part was the arguments in my romantic relationships. They would trigger intense emotions that would completely consume me. My emotions were spinning me around and around until I couldn't see any way out.

I'd go from feeling very intense to feeling very stupid as these emotional ups and downs continued. Every part of my life slowed down because I was basing my choices on how I felt rather than on what the evidence showed.

But then, things began to shift. It dawned on me that I could break free of the shackles of my feelings. I began to recognize the tales I was telling myself. This helped me distinguish these false narratives from the truth. It was then that I realized it was up to me to manage my feelings instead of allowing them to rule my actions.

It was a long and arduous journey but well worth it. I was able to break the cycle of negative self-talk and self-doubt by facing my emotions head-on. It all began when I realized I could choose how my feelings impacted me rather than letting them toss me around like a pinball.

My Genesis – Freedom Awakening

I remember the exact moment when I began to feel free. It was when I decided to quit my job as a makeup artist and pursue my true passion for entrepreneurship and service-based leadership.

At the time, I was plagued by fear and self-doubt. I had been told by others that my dreams were unrealistic and unattainable, and I began to believe them. But then, something inside me shifted.

I attended a self-development seminar called Landmark, led by the renowned speaker Gary Bishop. It proved to be a life-changing seminar for me. It was there that I started to untangle the web of lies and stories I had been telling myself. This allowed me to differentiate between facts and feelings.

The seminar was a transformative experience that helped me to confront my fears head-on. It taught me to challenge the stories I had been telling myself and to let go of the limiting beliefs that were holding me back.

After the seminar, I took a leap of faith and quit my job. It was scary, but it was also exhilarating. For the first time in a long time, I felt like I was in control of my life and my destiny.

That was the moment when fear began to transform into freedom. I realized that fear was not something to be avoided, but rather, it was something to be embraced and used as a source of motivation. Soon, I was able to achieve a level of freedom and fulfillment that I had never experienced before. I did that by facing my fears and challenging my limiting beliefs.

The journey from fear to freedom was not an easy one, but it was worth it. It was a journey of self-discovery and personal growth, and it has led me to where I am today. Now, I'm a successful entrepreneur who is passionate about helping others achieve their dreams.

Taking a Hit on Self-Worth

The first time my self-esteem was seriously dented as a business owner is a memory I will never forget. During my first contract, I had to organize events, provide sales consultations, and create content for an organization. One of my responsibilities was to ensure the success of an event they were hosting in Scottsdale, Arizona.

I expertly managed everything from tickets to payments to lanyards for 300 individuals. However, there were only about 150 attendees at the event itself. Even though my superiors never said anything bad about me, I still ended up tearing myself to pieces. My worst adversary was me. I constantly tore myself to shreds, convincing myself that I was unwelcome here.

The event was a tremendous success for the business, but I came away from it feeling like a total loser. At the time, I was a fanatic who demanded nothing less than absolute excellence. Hence, this caused me a great deal of stress. My self-esteem was plummeting because I had set an impossible bar for myself.

Reflecting on my past self, I recognize that I was too critical. As an entrepreneur, I've realized that setbacks are inevitable, and they don't need to characterize me. Reaching this realization was a process, but eventually, I learned to treat myself with compassion and forgiveness. Now, whenever my plans fall through, I tell myself it's fine to be human. I deserve to succeed despite the occasional setback.

Being Aware the Problem is 50% of the Work Done

Simply put, what is the problem? According to Tony Robbins, the problem is everything that's outside of your control or anything that doesn't conform to your plan.

In a famous quote, he says,

"The quality of your life is directly proportional to the amount of uncertainty you can comfortably live with."

This quote exemplifies his motivational style. If we "trade our expectations for appreciation," as he also says, every difficulty can be viewed as a chance for growth. In the face of adversity, we rise to the challenge and become better versions of ourselves. Life is not about returning to a previous state. Instead, it is about growing and improving in the present moment.

The purpose of adversity is to shake us out of the rut of our psychology, the reactive "monkey mind," which is automatic. Encountering difficulties breaks our habitual, subconscious routines. Difficulties are a part of being human. They're not an indication of our shortcomings or the "wrongness" of anything external to ourselves. They indicate that we are conscious beings having real experiences in the real world.

Temporary setbacks are essential for progress. They're not your fault, and these problems don't last forever. Pendulums always sway back. Challenges force us to grow as individuals and as a species. Darkness is necessary for light, sound for quiet, and development for stillness. Encountering and overcoming difficulties is an ongoing, lifelong practice.

Widely held belief has it that,

"A problem well-stated is a problem half-solved."

THE FEARLESS EXECUTIVE

This was said by Charles Kettering, the head of research at General Motors from 1920 to 1947 (Kotsides, 2022).

Even more famously, Albert Einstein once said,

"Given me one hour to save the world, I would spend 55 minutes defining the problem and 5 minutes finding the solution."

Even if the tone is over the top, the message is as relevant today as it was then. Our natural inclination, when presented with a problem, is to start thinking of ways to solve it. Nothing shocking there; on the contrary, leaders are characterized by decisiveness and action. But what, if anything, will these solutions fix if we don't know what the problem is? Could we be making matters worse by overlooking critical details?

Allow me to illustrate this with a straightforward case. A group arrives at a river and must cross to the other shore. They begin to propose routes across. They can walk through shallow water, go swimming, find a boat, or make a bridge. Of course, the success of any of these approaches depends on many variables.

Instead of immediately coming up with potential answers, they should be asking questions:

- Why are they going across?
- Do they need to transport anything with them?
- Does anyone know how deep the waterway is?
- Just how broad is it?
- Does everyone know how to swim?
- Is there access to boats or materials for constructing a bridge?

You get the idea. If they wade in and find that the water is too deep or the stream is too fast, they will have to retreat. If they start working on a bridge and then realize they don't have enough resources, they've wasted their time.

In this simple example, such questions may appear unnecessary. But as we all know, problems are rarely that easy, especially when they involve people from various parts of an organization. When we treat a problem as it appears on the surface and apply solutions without knowing the causes, we risk wasting time and resources. Who knows, we could end up introducing additional problems.

What can we do to stop this from happening? The solution lies in shifting our perspective on problem-solving. Don't rush into solving the problem; instead, take a step back and think it over carefully. In the same way that you might pause to think of questions as you cross a river, you should do the same thing here.

Tony Robbins is known for saying:

"Your biggest problem is you think you shouldn't have them. 'Cause problems are what make us grow. Problems are what sculpt our souls. Problems are what make us become more"

(Gatta, 2020)

It's fine to take things slowly so that we can fully grasp the situation. Even if we aren't Einstein and can't save the world, recognizing the problem is the first step in finding a solution. This concept allowed me to take a step back and experience greater freedom from panic and fear.

Facts Over Feelings

There are times when our feelings get the best of us, and we start to doubt our abilities. We let our imaginations run wild with these made-up stories and hypothetical situations. It's as if we're fooling ourselves into thinking the sky is plummeting when it's just a wisp of cloud. At these times, we must remember the strength that lies in truth.

Logical thinking and reasoning depend on facts. They are the unchanging truth that can help us center ourselves and return to reality when we stray from it. It's important to step back and evaluate what's true and what's not when we feel out of control emotionally.

For instance, some parents might feel like failures because of minor mishaps, such as giving their kid lunch a few minutes late. This feeling of failure isn't based on fact. All humans are fallible, and small mistakes like these are only natural. Instead of letting our feelings cloud our judgment, facing the facts can help us make more grounded decisions.

Therefore, we must have a firm grasp of the significance of the facts. Knowing the truth is only half the battle. You also need to be able to recognize when feelings are getting in the way of logic. When we can tell the truth from fiction, we're in a much better position to act in a way that supports our goals.

The Change Is Not Immediate but Painful

Sometimes life's transitions can feel jarring and out of the ordinary, but they're quite typical and necessary. Major life transitions occur with predictable frequency, even though each one is unique. A work by Bruce Feiler titled *Life Is in the Transitions: Mastering Change at Any Age* explores this idea. To write his book, he interviewed hundreds of people and discovered that on average, people undergo a significant life change every 12-18 months (Brooks, 2020). Three to five major ones, which Feiler names "life quakes," occur in almost everyone's lifetime.

The decision to get married or have a kid is an example of a voluntary and happy lifequake. Some, like joblessness or terminal disease, are unavoidable and never welcome. Large-scale collective changes frequently occur in variable forms. These include global events like the COVID-19 pandemic or shifts in culture.

Think about it: if you're just over thirty years old, you might have been born in 1990, right before the Soviet Union collapsed. When you were 11 years old, you witnessed the 9/11 attacks. You saw the global collapse of 2008 firsthand at the age of 18. The COVID-19 pandemic is currently underway. We can expect another catastrophic occurrence in the next decade, though we don't know what it will be.

Hard times have a way of drawing out people's creativity and resourcefulness. There's a lot written about "post-traumatic growth," a process by which people can benefit from upsetting experiences eventually. Learning from traumatic events by developing new traits like resilience, compassion, and a more profound sense of purpose in life is a net positive.

Some recent research suggests that increased inventiveness is another sign of this growth (Brooks, 2020).

During my transformation, I discovered a previously untapped source of creativity. Even during the pandemic, when I was already a prolific writer and speaker, my output increased drastically. The ease with which I can articulate novel ideas is inversely linked to my sense of security.

Life's transitions can hurt, but they're essential. Trying to fight these challenges instead of learning from them will only make things more difficult overall. Those who allow themselves to endure grim times gain the most from them. The best course of action is to embrace change as inevitable and make the most of it.

Takeaway

- Self-development is a long and arduous journey.
- With careful and consistent efforts, you can get to your goals.
- The four Fs of this chapter will make or break your success in this journey. Ditch fear, embrace freedom, and choose facts over feelings.
- Don't drive life with emotions at the wheel.
- Don't take a hit on self-worth because of external factors.
- Being aware of the problem is 50% of the work done.
- Change is not immediate but painful.

Chapter 2

Thoughts — Emotions — Actions: A Chain

"Courage is never to let your actions be influenced by your fears."

Arthur Koestler

Thoughts, emotions, and actions are all connected. Once you realize that your thoughts determine your emotions, you can use this knowledge to act in a certain way, which leads to more desirable outcomes. It's a domino effect known as "TFAR," which stands for "thoughts, feelings, actions, and

28

results." The cycle begins with your mental processes and ends with your behavior and outcomes.

Your beliefs become self-fulfilling when they're reinforced, transforming ideas into firm convictions. If you have strong beliefs, those ideas will direct your actions, which will in turn form habits. These habits can be positive or negative depending on the underlying belief. For example, believing health is important can lead to a habit of exercise, while believing your health doesn't matter can lead to a habit of skipping the gym.

Many people attempt to change the outcomes they dislike without first identifying and resolving the underlying factors that cause them. Those factors include values, attitudes, and emotions that contributed to those outcomes. If you're unhappy with your outcomes, first try to figure out why they're happening.

It's hard to tell when an idea is causing undesirable outcomes, particularly if you've been thinking a certain way for a long time. Negative thought patterns that contribute to bad outcomes become habitual. Being self-aware is the first step in modifying any behavior.

Changing Thoughts — A Pivotal Point

Let me spin you a yarn about overcoming fears and changing your thoughts. It all started when I was offered a job at a top-notch company, but the catch was I had to move to Arizona. No apartment, no friends or family, just me and my worries. But I didn't let that stop me. I grabbed that opportunity by the horns and began working there. With no place to crash in, I had to stay at a hotel. Nonetheless, I learned a lot from that company, which eventually helped me conquer my fears.

As if that wasn't enough, I even landed a contract with Bravo TV! I was on top of the world. Then, along came Tim. He was serious about me. But due to my previous experiences in toxic relationships, I wasn't interested in any romantic entanglements. Tim even wrote about his interest in his book, can you believe it? He was relentless in his pursuit and chased me to Florida.

This was a pivotal moment in my life when I had to make a choice. I could stay in my comfort zone, wallow in my low self-esteem and blame myself for every mistake, or take a chance and change everything. I chose the latter. I wanted to prove myself, to break free from my fears, and to learn more about the world. This opportunity was my golden ticket to shift from drama to data and take control of my life. And let me tell you, it was the best decision I ever made.

Taking Actions

For a long time, I've been doubtful of my abilities. I looked to others for inspiration and attempted to model my behavior after theirs. There are a lot of factors that separate successful people from unsuccessful people. But one primary distinction — willingness — has always stood out to me as the most important. Successful people are ready to put in the extra effort that their peers aren't.

That adage about following your passion and finding success is the most misunderstood concept I've ever come across. All around you, people are living and making decisions based on what "feels good." But they aren't moving any closer to the life they envision for themselves.

I remember feeling a bit lost and uncertain after moving to a new city. I knew that I wanted to do better for myself, but I wasn't sure how to go about it. This new opportunity was exciting and petrifying, but I decided to commit myself to it. Being the best was always an innate need for me, so I started looking for mentors who could guide me. And man, did I find some great ones!

One of my mentors introduced me to the **10x culture of Grant Cardone**, and I was instantly hooked. I loved his success formula and his message of taking massive action. I became a huge fan of his and started to incorporate his ideas into my own life.

That change helped me pick up good habits and routines to better myself every day. It also led me to work harder, focus more, and take more risks. I pushed myself to be the best that I could be, and it paid off.

Looking back, I'm glad that I took that chance and relocated for a better job opportunity. It led me to discover a whole new world of personal growth and development, and I'm a better person for it.

Setting the Bar High for Healthy Habits

Start raising the bar by taking baby steps and increasing your standards for yourself. Be thorough and remember where you are so you can recognize how far you've come later.

The word "success" is highly subjective. For some people, success implies financial gain. For others, it's about advancing their careers, or it may be a measure of how their job affects the world around them.

Everybody wants to make it big in life in the ways that matter to us. Most, however, fall short of our expectations for success. This is often the result of internal causes, such as the standards we impose upon ourselves. How do we go about changing this? Let me show you how. Start by doing little things that add up to big ones in your life.

The following is a rundown of things I emphasize in my life:

The Morning Routine

Having a schedule to follow every morning doesn't mean piling more work onto your plate. It's about making the most of your mornings to get the rest, relaxation, and mental clarity you need. That will help in tackling whatever the day brings.

Some of the best reasons to start your day with a routine are as follows:

- Better emotional and physical wellness
- Eases nerves and tension
- Increases concentration and motivation
- Reduces mental strain upon waking; promotes a sense of security, confidence, and stability
- Gives your day a framework to work within
- Allows you to plan your time more effectively
- Prepares you for success
- Encourages punctuality
- Boosts efficiency
- Enhances the standard of output

Setting up a good morning routine will benefit you with better moods, more energy, and lower stress level, which translates into getting more work done. Take time to refuel before the day's demands take their toll. A morning routine will help you to be better mentally, emotionally, and physically prepared to face the day's challenges.

Fill Your Mind with Positivity

Changing your existence begins with changing your mind, so fill it with good things. Here are some tips that may help you become more optimistic and, in turn, more productive.

Positive self-talk can set the tone for the entire day. How you begin each day is indicative of the type of day you will have. You know firsthand that when you get up late or in a panic, the remainder of the day is a wash. Starting the day in an awful mood often leads to carrying that disposition through the rest of the day. If you want to have a wonderful day, tell yourself as much when you look in the mirror. You won't believe how much better your day gets by doing something so absurd.

Think and speak positively to yourself. A "perfect day" does not exist. Therefore, prepare for fresh difficulties every day. Then, instead of whining about how hard things are, focus on solving the problems at hand. Use reassuring words to yourself to calm down. Repeat to yourself that everything is going to be fine and that you are handling it fine.

Find upbeat people to hang out with. It's common knowledge that being with optimistic people can improve your outlook on life. The more you take in uplifting language and anecdotes, the more they influence your thoughts. If you want to be a positive person, start by befriending other positive people.

Don't Just Go to Work; Go to Work to Succeed

Those who are effective go to work to achieve their goals. They put in extra time at the office to make their ambitions a reality. There's a powerful desire to get things done; one might even call it greed or selfishness, though there's nothing negative about this drive.

The saying "go to work to work" refers to the importance of showing up to your job to get real work done. The next step is to not just labor but to succeed, win, and take credit for what you've accomplished. Even though millions of people go to work every day, few of them have the right attitude or strategy to succeed.

Unsuccessful people have a stifling attitude toward their job. They speak negatively of their working lives. They use terms like the "daily grind" or "my life as a drone," among other expressions. Rather than seeing their job as a path to an abundant existence, they often whine about it. Enthusiasm for work changes your whole attitude. It makes it easier to focus and learn from the lessons of others, which cultivates success.

Be Motivated

The people I know who have achieved the most success are the ones who are willing to put in extra effort to get the task done and achieve their goals. They aren't distracted by the emotions of others or their doubts. They're motivated to put in the effort when others would instead take the easy route.

Unsuccessful people waste time allowing their feelings and thoughts to slow them down or convince them to settle for less than they deserve. Always be willing to go the extra mile, and you'll never be tempted to slack off and settle for second best.

No Excuses

Successful people know that no matter how many excuses they give, it won't change the result. Even good reasons for not doing something won't help if an important task never gets done.

Instead of making excuses, successful people view setbacks as learning experiences. They look at what went wrong and plan to do better next time. Unsuccessful people spend the same amount of time finding reasons why they haven't been able to achieve their goals. No matter how true any of these reasons may be, they won't help you find the motivation you need to overcome these challenges next time.

Concentration

The minds of the successful never wander from the goal. Morning goal-setting has been a ritual of mine for a long time now. When I put my mind to something, no matter how silly the result may seem, I always succeed. Create a mental image of yourself completing the goals you have set for yourself but have yet to achieve.

Those who don't succeed seem to let any distractions seep into their lives. What they concentrate on is out of their power. The typical American watches four hours of television per day, surfs the web for two, and makes a list of resolutions once a year (Valdivia, 2016). Imagine what you could be accomplishing in that time if you focused your efforts. No matter how big or small, every day is a fresh chance to make progress.

Read

According to one study, the most successful CEOs read more than 60 books per year, while the average American consumes just one (Valdivia, 2016). Most of Warren Buffet's time is spent reading. I still feel like I'm getting something special out of every book I read.

Some people might claim they "don't have time to read," but they're missing potentially life-changing information. Make time, whether you're sitting down with a book before bed or listening to an audiobook during your morning commute.

Impact on People Triggers Cashflow

It's simple to lose sight of the human element when discussing cash flow. However, a person's influence may not be measured in monetary terms, but rather in terms of the lives they touch.

Say that you run a modest enterprise selling handcrafted jewelry. The way you relate to your clientele is what will set you apart from the competition. Being dedicated to your craft or taking pleasure in making beautiful pieces is great, but it won't get you the sale. When you show genuine interest in your customers by learning about them and their tastes, your customer base is confident and loyal. This means more sales and more positive reviews.

Making a genuine link with your clientele is what generates revenue in this case. Customers return not just because they like what you're offering, but also because they feel heard and understood. Here, it stops being about money and starts being about people.

A leader in the community who gets people excited and involved is another example. They could improve their community by hosting events or holding fundraisers. There may be a domino effect of good prosperity because of their influence, which could bring in new business and investment. This has the potential to boost business activity, create new jobs, and expand the local economy.

In both cases, having a positive influence on others is profitable. Relationships and bonds between people are just as important as business deals. Whether it's a company, a community, or a cause, people are more apt to put in time and resources when they believe they are making a difference and are appreciated.

The Results

It's common knowledge that our decisions and actions can have far-reaching consequences. A difference in perspective can sometimes bring about dramatic improvements in our lives. This is what happened to me when I stopped looking for external validation. I began trusting in my abilities instead.

I used to put a lot of stock in what other people thought of me to boost my confidence. My lack of self-assurance led me to continually seek out criticism and affirmation. After retraining my mind to value myself more highly, however, I began to feel stronger. It felt like I was more in command of my life. My income also increased as a direct consequence.

This was not due to any sudden increase in my talent or proficiency. Rather, it was thanks to the fact that I had gained a newfound sense of certainty and pride in my abilities. Taking risks and stretching my abilities allowed me to expand my horizons.

The change in my outlook and behavior also affected my general health. I was less anxious and more at ease, which helped me pay more attention to other aspects of my life. It was a self-reinforcing cycle. My rising self-assurance led to greater accomplishments which in turn made me feel even better about myself.

Thus, changing our way of thinking and behaving can have far-reaching effects. Centering our thoughts on our value and confidence can help us access previously inaccessible possibilities and experiences. Living a life consistent with our principles and beliefs brings happiness that money can't buy.

<u>Takeaway</u>

- What you feed your mind will trigger emotions and result in actions.
- Start rewiring thoughts to change your emotions and actions for the better.
- Set the bar high for healthy habits.
- Have a morning routine.
- Fill your mind with positivity.
- Make an impact on people rather than focusing on dollars.

Chapter 3

Manage Your Mind

"Control your thoughts and everything will be under your control."

Debasish Mridha

Preface:

Parents do the best that they can with what they have. This chapter might have disturbing content for some parents. This is a polite reminder that nothing here is intended to hurt any parent. But instead, it is meant to offer clarity on different parenting perspectives that might scar a child for the rest of their life. No offense is intended.

When I was young, my mother's words would echo in my head:

"Be leery of that" and,
"Always have a plan B."

These statements changed the way I look at the world. The advice my mother gave me stuck with me as I explored my creative interests and worked toward my goals. As a freshman, I decided to try my hand at art courses in the hopes of discovering my inner artist. However, the constant barrage of negative feedback and rejection eventually broke me down. It was to the point where I had to seek refuge in the relative protection of nursing school.

Like my mother, my dad also harped on the importance of setting money aside for the future. Contrary to Grant Cardone's rule of boldness and total commitment, this was a strategy for playing it safe. As I got older, I understood that taking the safe route would not lead me to the life of my dreams.

My father, who had spent his life fearing and choosing the easy way out, came up to me at my brother's wedding. He confessed how incredible it was to see my brother and me making our own decisions and living our own lives. We had broken free of the chains of fear and dared to pursue our passions, creating our paths in life.

As an adult, I can see that my parents gave me unsuitable guidance when I was young. Being cautious and always having a backup plan may seem like a smart way to go through life. It makes us feel safe, but that safety is an illusion that keeps us from taking chances and developing to our maximum potential. It's better to abandon that sense of false safety as soon as you can. Face the uncertainties and dangers that life presents. This is the only way to uncover your true calling in life and achieve success on your terms.

Changing Frequency from the Inside

Energy is the building block of the universe, and humans are no exception. Everyone has their unique level of vibration. Every second of every day, all of us exchange energy with one another. As vibrational beings, we are not trained to behave as such. However, one of the best things you can do for yourself is to learn how to control your energy.

As opposed to many other aspects of living, your energy level is always under your control. You don't have to have faith in manifesting for it to work. You are already affecting the events that take place in your immediate environment. The only thing to consider is how content you are with the current state of things. You have every right to be angry about frustrating situations when dealing with the outside world. But don't let your anger get the best of you; it won't accomplish anything.

Inside is where it all starts to unfold. The universe will pick up on your vibes. To top it all off, you have a complete say over what kind of energy you put into the universe. Every one of us seeks contentment and serenity. Yet, without even recognizing it, we can unintentionally move away from these objectives through the decisions we make every day. It's simple and difficult at the same time to make decisions that bring us closer to our goals.

Many Small Changes = Big Changes

Now that you know the importance of changing your frequency, you may be pondering how to do so. This is by no means an all-inclusive list.

But following even a few of the suggestions here will have a positive effect on your mood.

- Imagine what the future holds in store for you
- Tune in
- Practice meditation
- Practice thankfulness
- Be wary of how much negative media you interact with
- Reduce your caffeine intake

- Maintain a mindful attitude
- Think about things that make you happy

Cognitive Dissonance

If what you do doesn't match what you believe, you can feel uncomfortable. This feeling is called cognitive dissonance. For example, a person who knows that smoking is bad for their health might feel better when they smoke, but later they feel bad for doing it. This is because their beliefs and feelings don't match up.

The things we learn and experience as children profoundly impact what we stand for as adults. These ideas originate from national norms, family traditions, and general social consensus. When our ideal selves are at odds with our current selves, we may struggle with cognitive conflict as we develop into adulthood.

It's not easy to overcome the generational curses and ingrained social norms that we've all been exposed to since childhood. The internal conflict caused by trying to change one's mind about these things is a potential trigger for an identity crisis. It takes bravery to question these beliefs. By working on ourselves and taking positive steps, we can learn to control our feelings and overcome our fears about the future.

There are some things we have been told that may not be true or appropriate for us, and it's important to recognize them. It takes courage and resolve to reject an untrue narrative and refuse to take part in it. To live a satisfying life, we must work on personal growth and take steps to match our beliefs with who we are. This includes overcoming cognitive dissonance. Hence, if you're currently experiencing this state, do yourself a favor and break free from those chains. Embrace yourself fully and acknowledge your potential. Take those necessary steps to go after what you truly desire.

Relationship with God — Going Back to Faith and Scripture

As a child, I was instilled with the belief that I must obey established laws and faith beliefs. I've felt trapped by the constraints of the standards my family and society have set for me. My Christian upbringing, however, also instilled in me the value of reflection and a quest for self-improvement.

I went on a spiritual retreat once, seeking refuge in my beliefs. There, I had an epiphany: my faith could be a vehicle for self-discovery rather than a means of subjugation. I began rereading sacred texts with the realization that my faith was not merely a set of dogmas to be obeyed, but rather a personal connection with a higher force. This fresh outlook gave me the confidence to go against social mores that had been instilled in me from an early age.

A series of baby steps, including speaking up and exercising more independence in my decision-making, led to a major shift in my life. My religious beliefs gave me the fortitude to persevere through hardships, including challenges and disapproval from the world. I had to follow my heart and believe in my intuition because my spiritual path was different from anyone else's.

Today, I'm happy to say that I'm no longer confined by my past. My religious beliefs have been and will continue to be, instrumental in my quest for self-improvement and independence.

Snapping Out of It

The pressure of my family's lofty standards had been crushing me for a long time. Success, in their eyes, meant choosing a career that didn't include my ambition to become a writer. I felt like I was being held captive in a world that was not meant for me. But even when life gets tough, fate will amaze you with its power.

After having my epiphany and moving past my family's advice, I started pursuing a better job, and doors opened for me. Even though I'd been told I couldn't make money as a writer, I was writing content for Bravo TV and loving it.

Although this was a minor act of defiance, it represented a huge step toward independence. Writing helped me spread my wings. The more I pursued my interest in writing, the clearer it became to me that I could be anything I wanted to be.

Regardless of what my family thought, I didn't have to let their views on the world dictate my outlook on life. Not everyone supported me or my decisions, and that made it tough. But I persisted, and with each new day came a feeling of freedom I'd never known before.

Now that I've matured, I can see that my parents' goal was for me to unlock my potential and pursue my passions. Unfortunately, I had my wings clipped, preventing me from reaching my full potential. Breaking those family superstitions was the turning point that allowed me to see my true potential. Everything I've had is because I finally let go and stopped tying myself down.

Don't Have a Plan B

Many successful people advocate for having no backup plans. This is because having a fallback can act as a psychological crutch. It can hinder your dedication to your goal. If you're always thinking about what to do if something goes wrong, you won't be able to focus on how to achieve your intended outcome. Eventually, this could restrict your capabilities and reduce your odds of success.

Besides, being unprepared for failure forces you to face your fears and depend solely on your resources. It teaches you to be resourceful when faced with difficulties. It inspires you to look outside the box. Having this frame of mind can be extremely useful in life because it compels you to overcome obstacles and develop resilience and flexibility.

One of the main advantages of not having a backup plan is the increased concentration that comes with it. When you can always fall back on an escape plan, it's easy to get sidetracked and lose perspective of your goal. Taking away that cushion forces you to prioritize your objectives. Having laser-like concentration improves your odds of success.

Watch Your Inner Dialogue

How we talk to ourselves has a major bearing on our state of mind, self-esteem, and general happiness. Our inner dialogue can either fuel our success or interfere with it. Keeping an eye on your internal dialogue is important because you want to make sure you're encouraging and inspiring yourself. Negative self-talk has the potential to manifest into reality.

Low self-esteem from negative internal dialogue can prevent us from taking necessary risks. By comparison, practicing positive self-talk can help in the development of resilience and a solid sense of identity. Furthermore, the words we say to ourselves can shape the way we see the universe. Constant self-criticism can lead to increased cynicism about others and the world.

A pessimistic perspective on life is harmful to our psychological well-being. If we pay attention to our thoughts, we can change our unfavorable thought processes for positive ones. We can train ourselves to recognize and reject destructive self-talk, then replace it with loving and accepting statements. Ensure your inner dialogue is a positive one. This will provide the boost that is needed to succeed in life.

Find the Why in Your Low Frequency

Understanding the "why" behind your lower-frequency moods is essential. It often points to a deeper problem with origins in beliefs formed as a kid. It could also be a byproduct of a generational curse. When you find the underlying cause of what's making you feel or act a certain way, you can start to make changes.

Upbringing and early life experiences influence many of our core values and habits. Beliefs formed in early life can have a lasting impact on how we feel, think, and behave as adults. Taking the time to see our inner world through the lens of our feelings allows us to recognize the limiting beliefs. This also helps in seeing the negative self-talk that may be holding us back. Address any underlying issues that lead to negative emotions or behaviors and break generational curses, ensuring you won't pass them down to your kids.

Learning to question our ingrained beliefs can help us develop into better versions of ourselves. Moreover, figuring out the "why" behind your lower frequencies can motivate you to make constructive changes. This makes room in your life for better experiences. This opens you up to better relationships that support your goals and ideals. As you develop your full potential and follow your goals, your life gets more rewarding and purposeful.

Thought Auditing

Don't get overwhelmed by the idea of auditing your thoughts. Just consider it innocent curiosity. Are you prepared to face the truth about your difficulties and make a fresh start? I had to go through a lot of suffering before I could say, "Alright, this wasn't right for me."

What would you want to change about your own life?

- How do you feel first thing in the morning?
- Do you enjoy what you do for a living?
- Have you been enjoying your relationships?

- Do you feel like you're making a difference in the world?

If you answered "no" to any of the above questions, make a change now. Have you ever taken the time to think critically about your thought processes? Examine your inner dialogue and weed out the naysaying.

Here are three simple ways to check your thinking:

1. Take a sheet of paper and jot down as many of your thoughts as you can for a few minutes. Don't read them and don't try to force your opinions. Everything must come naturally.
2. Once you've finished, review what you have written.
3. Devote ten minutes to writing down some "positive truths," and then review what you have written three times.

Do you feel how much more uplifting your thoughts are when you consciously focus on positivity? The term "feel" is essential. It helps to feel encouraging remarks, even if they are coming from within your head. This method is one that I use frequently. When I'm feeling down, I do a mental health checkup and try to use positive self-talk to get better. This simple tactic works every time. Try it out whenever you need a little boost.

<u>Takeaway</u>

- You have every right to live out the wildest of dreams.
- You are blinded from seeing those dreams by the limits and beliefs stored in your subconscious.
- Bring about the change you seek by working on yourself from the inside out, beginning with your thoughts and ideas.
- Don't have a plan B.
- Snap out of generational curses.
- Watch your inner dialogue.
- Find the why in your lower frequency.
- Perform thought auditing.

Chapter 4

Confidence is Key

"No one can make you feel inferior without your consent."

Eleanor Roosevelt

I used to have trouble understanding how people could navigate life without fear. How can they converse with their superiors as if they were their employee? How did they work up the nerve to ask out an amazing girl on a date? How can they speak in front of an audience? A single term sums up the response to these questions: "confidence." You can't fake success, and confidence is essential to achieving it. This means everyone who's working toward success is trying to boost their self-confidence.

We tend to blame ourselves when we fall short of expectations, telling ourselves things like, "I failed at this" or "I'm just not that successful." But here's something to think about what if we fell into a trap? It's not that you're flawed. It's just that you don't know how to play the confidence game, either because you never gave it any thought or because society gave you the wrong guidelines to play it. Even if violating these unspoken rules yielded temporary benefits for us, they weren't enough to meet our needs. So, what's the right way to play?

Why should you put so much trust in yourself? The answer is simple: trust is vital if we are to achieve our goal of making positive changes in our lives. For the sake of completing our top goals, or to boost performance in a specific area, confidence is key. Let's look at how you can build confidence.

Keeping Your Promises to Yourself

Many of us associate keeping a promise with our commitment to others. This commitment could be to a friend, a spouse, a loved one, or a current or potential job. Keeping our word is a fantastic way to show that we care about others and about the things they value, such as dependability, credibility, ability to compromise, and integrity.

THE FEARLESS EXECUTIVE

To ensure that we can keep our promises, we must carefully consider our schedules, commitments, and resources. When a promise is not kept, it can cause feelings of sadness and anger for the person on the receiving end. If we examine our intentions, we may find that we avoid breaking promises because we don't want the other person to feel bad.

Keeping our word to others is essential to any healthy connection. However, keeping our word to ourselves is just as—if not more—crucial. Keeping our promise can boost our sense of agency, purpose, and self-assurance.

Confidence is based on trust, which in turn is based on the firm conviction that another person is trustworthy, truthful, able, or powerful. We show our reliability as trustworthy person who keeps their word. We can count on ourselves when we make a promise to ourselves and keep it. When we learn to rely on ourselves to follow through, we gain the confidence that comes from knowing we can be counted on.

Saying something and not doing it chips away at your confidence. When you tell yourself lies, you cease having faith in who you are. When you lose faith in yourself, others will lose faith in you as well. Therefore, when you make a vow, get it done. Whatever you promise yourself, make sure you follow through to the end.

Why People Lose Confidence

I've been in the coaching and executive development industry for several years. Therefore, I can attest to the fact that losing confidence is a common struggle for many professionals. Our company, called the Executive Career Upgrade, is designed to help executives reach their full potential.

At the start of this program, I was excited to be surrounded by executives at the top of their game exactly as I had envisioned. However, I soon realized that many of these executives were struggling with self-confidence. They were emotionally overdriven. This came as a shock to me. But it also made me realize that we needed to include a mindset part in our program to help address this issue.

This realization pushed me toward my goal of learning how to boost my confidence. Many of the leaders I was collaborating with had lost confidence due to their upbringing. They also lost confidence because of working their way up the corporate hierarchy. Some suffered setbacks like being fired after decades of service, working in a toxic environment, receiving low pay, or being confined to a single role. Many top-level executives lacked the confidence that came from knowing their true value.

Since I started Executive Career Upgrade, I've gained a better understanding of why it's crucial to focus on mental toughness and confidence. Our company provides tools to professionals to boost their confidence and overcome their limiting beliefs. These tools enable them to do wonderful things in their careers and personal life.

Tools for Being Confident

To develop confidence, practice optimistic self-talk. Create mental images of yourself succeeding.

Concentrate on your best qualities to increase your self-assurance. No one has all the answers, so it's okay to search them out; in fact, doing so can be seen as a sign of strength.

Having Personal Brand

Apart from having a strong character, having a good reputation in your professional field can make you an unbeatable force. How others evaluate you and your abilities is your brand. Building a solid identity for yourself allows you to highlight your skills and set yourself apart from the competition.

Knowing yourself and your strengths can help you feel more confident in professional situations like employment interviews, networking events, and presentations. You'll have the wherewithal to face these circumstances with the knowledge that you're contributing something of value.

Determine what makes you stand out from the crowd. Then use that information to craft a consistent statement that promotes your brand through online and in-person networking activities.

Having Tactics and Strategies

Having a strategy to get where you want to go professionally is crucial. SMART (Specific, Measurable, Achievable, Relevant, and Time-bound) goal setting is a detailed plan outlining each step of creating a realistic goal. The SMART goal-setting method also ensures you have a deadline for completion, which encourages motivation and dedication. You won't feel as confused or unsure of yourself when you have a plan for getting where you want to go. Instead, you can zero in on specific measures that will bring you closer to your goal. Be flexible and willing to adjust your strategy as you move forward in your work.

Understanding the Market's Perception of Success

It's crucial to recognize how your accomplishments resonate with your intended audience. What are the most sought-after qualities and experiences of businesses and consumers? If you have this knowledge, you will be in a better position to promote your skills to prospective employers. You'll feel more assured and set yourself apart from the pack.

Fear and Imposter Syndrome

Many people suffer from fear of failure at some time in their careers. If you don't learn to control these emotions, they can hold you back.

We experience fear as a normal reaction to anything we judge to be dangerous or unclear. You might fear taking on something new because you're worried about making mistakes. Or you might be worried about finding a job that's a good fit for your interests and abilities. These fears can be so overwhelming that you put off work or a job hunt. They lead you to avoid taking risks or accept less than you deserve.

Imposter syndrome is another prevalent experience that can derail your professional life. It's the belief that your qualifications or competence are overstated despite objective evidence to the contrary. You may start to feel like an imposter if you're only trying to be competent in your position. This can lead you to question your abilities, understate your achievements, and pass up chances to improve your situation.

How do you get past the imposter syndrome and any doubts you have about your abilities? The first step is to recognize and accept these emotions as part of the typical human experience. Fear and uncertainty are normal human emotions; what matters is how you deal with them.

Motivating and encouraging oneself through self-compassion and affirmative speech is another useful tactic. Be as supportive and encouraging to yourself as you would be to a buddy. Focus on the positives by reminding yourself of your skills, experience, and contributions.

Finally, find someone who has been through a comparable situation. Look to them for guidance and support. If you're struggling to overcome feelings of imposter syndrome, ask how others overcame these doubts in their lives, and try to follow suit.

Never let doubt or impostor syndrome prevent you from achieving your professional goals. Boost your self-confidence and move closer to your professional goals when you allow yourself to experience these emotions. Show yourself compassion and reach out for help.

Build a Battle Plan

You shouldn't go into your job without a strategy, just as a general wouldn't go into battle without a plan of action.

What makes a well-thought-out strategy so crucial? For one thing, it lets you anticipate problems rather than just deal with them after the fact. You'll be better prepared to deal with challenges and difficulties if you already know what you want and how to get it. Instead of playing catch-up, you can foresee difficulties and work out solutions in advance.

Making a strategy also helps keep your mind and spirit focused. With so many things to do and places to go in your professional life, it's easy to lose focus or feel stressed. But if you divide your plan into manageable chunks, you can start each day with enthusiasm and optimism.

How do you go about devising a strategy to advance your professional standing? Determine your ultimate professional aspirations first. Where do you see yourself in 5, 10, or 20 years? Once you know what you want to accomplish, you can set goals for shorter time limits like a year or a few months.

Determine what you'll need to succeed, what you can expect to get in your way, and what you'll have to do at each stage of the plan. This could mean learning something new, making connections in your field, or looking for new employment. It's essential to keep in mind that career planning is a continuous process, not a one-and-done task. To make sure you are continuously moving in the right direction, it's important to regularly set goals and review your strategies.

Rebuilding Thoughts Before Job Mapping

For many, the stress of working in corporate America is one of life's greatest difficulties. Many people experience exhaustion, stress, and dissatisfaction due to stressful aspects of the workplace, such as a fast-paced environment or a cutthroat atmosphere.

The first step in solving any issue is to step back and examine the situation objectively. Whether it's finding a job or climbing the corporate ladder, identify what's keeping you from your goals. Are you lacking a certain skill? Is it just surface-level dissatisfaction? Perhaps a bad working environment, or past trauma or burnout, is making it harder to focus?

People often struggle with feelings of helplessness, dissatisfaction, and misery at work. This can occur when an employee doesn't feel their contributions are valued when they don't have sufficient say over their work, or when their values and those of the business are at odds.

To get ahead of these obstacles, you need a new perspective on your job hunt and professional growth. This could mean looking for guidance from a career coach or mentor. Also, reassess your values and goals. One more thing is to research career tracks that better suit your interests and abilities.

Taking responsibility for your professional development is the ultimate key to a satisfying job. You can land a job that is a good fit for you and your goals by being realistic about your abilities, your dreams, and the things that drive and inspire you.

People Aren't Happy

Confidence comes from having clear targets in your life. Stumbling blindly through the dark woods is scary, but once you see the light at the end, there's nothing to fear. Unfortunately, people don't seem to have a clear sense of direction anymore, which is making them unhappy. Look at the following stats.

Statistics That Matter When Discussing Job Satisfaction

- In 2022, 60% of workers were mentally detached, and 19% were miserable.
- 72% of employees say that having respect for others in the workplace is critical to their happiness.
- After a coworker issue, 16% would quit.
- Employee turnover rates average around two to three years per position.

Many people all around the world are not happy with their jobs, and this can make them feel bad about work and less productive. However, employers who take time to find out why their employees aren't happy can make things better for everyone. They can take steps to improve the mood and satisfaction of their employees at work, which supports the whole team's success.

Envision Your Ideal Future

Everyone must ask themselves "What next?" at some point in their careers. Though we all get there at our speed and in our ways, this junction in the road is often a time of reckoning. It could happen right when you're about to embark on a new chapter of your life, such as when you're about to graduate and have the "prepared to take the bull by the horns" mentality. It can also manifest during a particularly trying moment, like when you're moving across the country.

When everything feels out of order, and you feel like you've lost your grip, there's nothing to fear. Even in despair, inspiration can strike. A clear image of what's to come will help you not just manage uncertainty, but also inspire and guide you.

"It Won't Be Any Different Tomorrow" — Is this True Though?

Too many of us believe in the "why do today what you can put off until tomorrow" mentality. If you tend to disregard the next day as unremarkable, you may never recognize the significance of planning for the future. On the other hand, perhaps you're already thinking about your future, but haven't yet found a way to live up to your maximum potential.

Of course, writing down your life's goals is no guarantee that you'll achieve them. Plenty of people lead fulfilling lives without ever putting pen to paper. Others have journals filled with ideas but no drive to follow through on them.

Still, putting your goals down in writing is a key step. It helps you prevent potential roadblocks that could derail your progress toward your long-term objectives. There's a saying, "Even a blind squirrel finds a nut now and then." Many individuals have undoubtedly become prosperous in this manner. But wouldn't you rather "develop" your successes than take a chance on "finding" them?

Become a Problem Solver

I had the opportunity to work with a client who had moved to a new country and was experiencing a lot of anxiety related to his race. He grew up in a culture where certain beliefs and habits were deeply ingrained. That made it difficult for him to let go of limiting thoughts and behaviors that were holding him back.

Despite these challenges, he was determined to make a change. Unlike many of our clients, he took massive action within just 90 days of our first meeting. It was inspiring to witness his transformation as he worked hard to rebuild his belief systems. He broke free from the generational curses that had been holding him back.

Through his hard work and persistence, he was able to achieve a new level of career success that no one in his family had ever achieved before. He did it all with grace and courage, despite the many obstacles that stood in his way.

I'm proud to say that my client landed a coveted job in the finance department of Bank of America. It wasn't easy. He had to network extensively within the industry and put himself in front of some very influential people. But he persevered, and his hard work paid off in the end.

Working with clients like this one is truly what makes my job so rewarding. It's amazing to see how a little guidance and support can help someone overcome even the most challenging obstacles and achieve their dreams.

99% of our clients come to us with zero confidence. But we help them build that confidence and give them the mindset of becoming a problem solver.

My Definition of Confidence

Confidence serves as the catalyst for both personal and professional development. It's the willingness to try new things, work toward our maximum potential, and take steps to better ourselves. Those who lack confidence report feeling stuck, with no motivation to change their circumstances.

Confidence can be cultivated through the practice of asking yourself questions daily:

- Are you growing?
- Are you moving?
- Are you keeping those promises?
- Are you happy with the person you see in the mirror?

These questions serve as useful reminders to keep our eyes on the prize. Not everyone is born with confidence. It may take a lot of effort and experience for some people to achieve the confidence they need to thrive in a professional setting. A positive outlook and a willingness to try new things will make the process easier.

Don't give up if you're having self-esteem issues. Always keep in mind that progress toward your goals is progress toward your best self. With time and effort, your confidence will increase, and you'll discover that you're capable of more than you ever imagined.

The Happiness Theory by Jordan Peterson

Canadian psychologist, author, and psychology lecturer Jordan Peterson has a theory about what makes us happy.

He argues in his book *12 Rules for Life: An Antidote to Chaos* that knowing you're making progress toward a goal is the key to happiness.

Peterson claims that seeking meaning and purpose through the accomplishment of objectives is a natural human state. It's easy to feel aimless, bewildered, and unfulfilled if we don't have anything to guide us.

According to Peterson, happiness is not a fixed destination but rather a path to be traveled. It's not so much about getting somewhere as it is about getting somewhere closer. This means that if we believe we are making progress toward our objectives, we can still feel happiness and satisfaction (Peterson, 2018).

Peterson's idea is a rallying cry for us to get up and go after what we want out of life. Doing so can help us feel like our lives have significance and direction, which is a prerequisite for experiencing happiness and fulfillment.

<u>Takeaway</u>

- Confidence is the ultimate key for your advancement in life and a core skill that is non-negotiable in all aspects of life.
- Keep your promises to yourself.
- Have a personal brand.
- Have strategies in place.

- Envision your ideal future.
- Become a problem solver.

Chapter 5

Success Needs Support

"Encourage, lift, and strengthen one another. For the positive energy spread to one will be felt by us all. For we are connected, one and all."

Deborah Day

As I stood outside of Cardone Ventures with Tim, I couldn't help but feel a mixture of excitement and anxiety. We were considering making the biggest investment we had ever made in our business, but we didn't have the cash lying around. We knew that we needed to come up with a creative solution to make this half a million-dollar investment in our business a reality.

It wasn't about the money, though. We knew the importance of being around people who were living the same life that we aspired to, both in our personal and professional lives. We needed to invest in people who had a genuine interest in pushing us toward our goals.

When we finally made the decision to invest in Cardone Ventures, it was a momentous change for our business. Brandon Dawson, one of the consultants who worked with us, had a way of disarming me and exposing the areas where I lacked knowledge and focus. It was a humbling experience, but it also gave me the opportunity to get the help and support that I needed.

Not Knowing Everything About Your Business is Okay

Working with mentors and coaches like the team at Cardone Ventures allowed us to take a step back and really analyze our business. We had consultants come into each area of our business and analyze our sales, finance, marketing, and more. They gave us extra sets of eyes and helped us identify areas where we were ignoring key details.

Mentors and trainers are helpful because they often see opportunities that you miss. They are objective because they have no personal investment in the company and can examine it from an outsider's perspective. Together, you'll be able to pinpoint weak spots in your business. Mentors allow you to receive the expert advice and resources you need to grow your company to the next level.

Getting On the Same Page as Your Spouse

The process of working with Cardone Ventures also brought Tim and me together on the same page. We were able to break our business plan into smaller, more manageable parts. We identified the necessary steps that we needed to take for the growth and expansion of our business. We made sure not to move too quickly to avoid potential breakdowns in certain areas.

Getting on the same page with your spouse is crucial for your relationship and business. Elena Cardone, the wife of successful international speaker, entrepreneur and author, Grant Cardone, is a vocal proponent of this idea. She has written many speeches on the importance of being on the same page as your significant other.

Having a common goal for the future is at the heart of what it means to "get on the same page." Collaborating on a shared vision and strategy for success is essential. To do this, you must be open and honest about your capabilities and limitations. Devise means of mutually bolstering your efforts.

Elena's hypothesis hinges, in part, on the efficacy of dialogue. To find common ground with your partner, having frank and open conversations about your desires and worries is important. This requires the ability to open up and listen, even if you disagree with your partner.

Having a set of ideals in common is also crucial. This means that you and your partner should share similar values about what is most significant in life. You can move together toward your goals by agreeing on a core collection of principles.

Elena concludes by stressing the value of staying with one another through the good and tough times. Support one another through difficult moments and rejoice in one another's achievements. You can do far more as a team than you could ever hope to do individually.

Not Seeking Help is a Sign of Weakness

Although many would have you think otherwise, asking for help is a sign of strength, not one of weakness. It requires bravery and vulnerability to acknowledge that you are struggling and that you could benefit from help. It's about admitting you don't know everything and being open to learning from others.

On the other hand, refusing to ask for help may indicate arrogance or obstinacy. It can cause more stress and burnout. Refusing to ask for help can minimize chances for personal development.

Many of us have experienced feelings of exhaustion and isolation that result from trying to go it alone. Asking for help can help you regain control in these situations. Letting others lend a hand means better success and happiness in both our professional and personal lives. Whether you're seeking advice from a mentor, consulting a therapist, or working with colleagues on a project, allow others to help when needed.

Everyone needs help at some point along the way, and it's perfectly normal to ask for it. Admitting we need help is an act of fortitude and courage. It can be a highly effective means of overcoming obstacles and realizing our goals. Thus, never be afraid or embarrassed to ask for help.

Holistic Health Approach

Tim and I strongly believe in the value of having a personal coach. It's like having a dependable GPS that effortlessly leads us to our final location. Whether it's a question of marriage, health, or work, we always have someone to turn to for counsel.

Preventive repair is highly valued because of the time and money it can save us overall. We are proactive in our personal and business lives, as we are with our cars, which we service regularly. Similarly, we make it a habit to check in with a coach routinely rather than waiting for issues to emerge.

Our mentors are reliable allies in our pursuit of excellence. They give us the resources and methods to overcome the obstacles we face. Having a life coach helps us stay on track and accomplish our goals.

Don't sit around waiting for issues to arise before you get help. Take a holistic view of your health. Hire a counselor in every area of your life to maximize your potential and return on investment. When you do this, you'll be astounded at how much easier the ride becomes.

Building Leadership Culture

In the entrepreneurial world, it's easy to get caught up in an illusion. People think that they can solve every problem on their own. But the truth is that as the business expands, it gets harder and harder to handle everything on their own. This is where developing a mindset of leadership comes into play.

Your company's success depends on the quality of the leadership team you've assembled. A managerial team enables you to focus on your strengths while they manage other parts of the business.

Developing a leadership culture also involves instilling a feeling of mutual obligation. Couple that with taking pride in team members. This not only increases responsibility but also encourages teamwork and camaraderie. To encourage employees to take personal interest in the company's success, let your staff take responsibility for their work.

To be an effective leader, give your team the tools they need to achieve their goals. This means letting them make decisions and offering support during tough times. You must also provide them with opportunities for ongoing learning and growth. By investing in your team, you can ensure the long-term success of your company.

No company can thrive without a strong leadership mindset. Build a dedicated team capable of managing various aspects of your company. Pay them well and instill a sense of shared responsibility and ownership in them. This fosters a cooperative and helpful workplace culture.

<u>Takeaway</u>

- Investing in your business by hiring mentors and trainers may seem scary, but it can benefit your company's success.
- Investing in your business can help you identify your weaknesses, inspire you to achieve your goals, and guide you toward the resources necessary for success.

- It might be time to find a mentor or coach if you're at a standstill in your business or have doubts about its future.
- Not micromanaging everything about your business is okay.
- Get on the same page as your spouse.
- Not seeking help is a sign of weakness.
- Build leadership culture.

Chapter 6

Fear is the Real Plague in America

"Fear is pain arising from the anticipation of evil."

Aristotle

People often let fear prevent them from taking risks and realizing their potential. Fear is a significant deterrent to people considering leaving a stable corporate position to pursue entrepreneurship. They hesitate because they're afraid of the potential consequences of taking a leap, including but not limited to failing, losing money, or making a mistake.

But remember that you can overcome your fears and move forward with your goals despite them. Fear can be channeled into action to help you achieve your goals. When you face your worries head-on, you can use them to fuel your drive to achieve your goals.

In this chapter, we'll investigate why some people hesitate to quit their 9-to-5s even when they have dreams of entrepreneurship. We'll talk about how social responsibility influences their choices and how to deal with the toxic corporate culture in America. We'll also look at the recipe for overcoming fear and succeeding.

The Driving Force of Fear

People's obsession with the news stems from their own anxieties. That is both hilarious and illuminating. I have a neighbor who I rarely talk to. Every morning, while it's still dark outside, I see his big screen playing whatever news channel it is - NBC or MS-something. He's glued to the screen day and night, and it just baffles me. However, it also serves as a great reminder that I'm doing something different with my day. Instead of being swayed by a continuous stream of bad news, I concentrate on doing good in the world. I decide where I expend my energy and what information I absorb.

Seeing other people's lives ruled by fear makes me appreciate how lucky I am to have avoided that way of life. Perhaps there are people who have never been caught in such a snare, but I was. When I finally broke the habit of worrying about everything, it was like a weight had been lifted off my shoulders. I thank God every morning that I broke free of that narrative of fear.

I can recall a time when I was almost pulled into a scary narrative - it was when I gave birth to my son. Naturally, I wanted to shield him from harm. And the nature and potential consequences of that deadly virus were unknown. But then I realized that fear almost overwhelmed me. Constantly listening to the news is exhausting, limiting, and a fear-driven behavior. This brand-new form of confinement isn't one I wish to participate in.

Seeing through my neighbor's window in the morning is a beautiful visual reinforcement that I've made the right decision for my health and mental wellbeing. It reminds me to not watch the media. I won't fill my mind with negativity outside of my control. To change the world; I have to focus on my own area of influence and master that. We must stop letting worries about the future control our actions in the here and now.

Stay in Your Lane

As we go about our daily lives, we are bombarded with a never-ending tide of data, commentary, and analysis. Nowadays, getting lost in the sea of information is easy simply because there's simply too much of it. Staying where you belong has always been important. But in today's world, it's more important than ever to do just that. This is more than a bit of advice. It's a gentle reminder that sometimes the best way to overcome fear is to keep doing what you've always done.

The continuous tide of shocking news that fills our screens can be overwhelming. It's normal to feel powerless and hopeless in the face of such devastation and disorder. The fact that we do have an option, however, cannot be ignored. It is up to us to decide whether we will let dread rule our minds and bodies.

To stay on the right track, a person must be aware of where their attention and energy are going. Focusing on the things over which you have some measure of control and influence is different from choosing to ignore the issues facing the world. It's about making your own choices in life and not allowing other people or circumstances to influence you.

By not trying to spend your energy saving the world, you'll have more time and energy to devote to your own goals. The same is true of judging your success by its own merits, and not trying to compete with anyone else. You're not racing against anyone or even attempting to match their pace. You're not trying to impress anyone; you're just doing your best.

Staying on your chosen path is about more than achieving your personal success or goals. It's also about finding your own method to positively impact the world. Each of us can contribute to the greater good by making use of our unique set of knowledge, abilities, and interests. In our own ways, we can make an impact in the world, whether through activism, volunteering, or even being a good friend.

To stay on your own path is to be authentic. Being true to yourself and the values you uphold is essential. Decide how you want to live your existence and don't let anyone tell you otherwise. Being authentic allows you to build an existence that you love and enjoy.

A Sense of Responsibility

It's easy to get discouraged by the current condition of the world and believe that problems are beyond our ability to solve. But that doesn't mean we don't have responsibilities to fulfill while we're here. While I recognize that there are those who don't think it's their job to change the world, I'm confident in saying that we all shape our communities. Everyone has something valuable to contribute, whether their goal is global change or local community building.

My friend, for example, believes that her true purpose is to support and uplift those around her every day. It's not a showy or dramatic way to make an impact, but it's lovely, nonetheless. On the other hand, I'm determined to use our business to effect positive change in the world. It's not how much of an effect we have that matters, but simply that we act and do what we can to improve the world while we are here.

Therefore, don't become disheartened by the magnitude of the difficulties we must overcome. Let's instead center our attention on the here-and-now actions we can take to make a change.

Recognizing Fear in Corporate America

It hit me like a ton of bricks when I realized that fear is the ultimate corporate disease. Here I am, running my Executive Career Upgrade business, enrolling people left and right into my program to help them land their dream job. I know all the job search tactics there are to know - I'm a real job search expert. But what I didn't expect was that the biggest hurdle for these folks wasn't their resume or interview skills. It was their mindset.

See, these people are beat down. They've been through the ringer in toxic work environments, clawing their way up the corporate ladder only to get the rug pulled out from under them. It's downright traumatizing. And here's the kicker - these are the supposed "leaders" of Corporate America. They're CEOs of major companies, the cream of the crop. And they're a mess.

I'll be honest with you, it's a scary realization. I used to think these CEOs were the best of the best. It turns out that they're just as human as the rest of us. They're doubting themselves, making questionable decisions, and second-guessing every move they make.

What's even sadder is that they have little to no self-worth despite their financial success. I've had clients who look like they have it all together on paper. They'll be a CEO of some bigwig company, raking in the dough. Later, I find out they're barely keeping their head above water. Many are divorced, depressed, and forced to tap into their 401K. Some have even taken their own life. Recognizing how many CEOs struggle with these issues is a tough pill to swallow.

But that's where my program comes in. I've had to build a whole course just to help these folks get their heads straight. We work on their mindset and goals, step by step, for a solid 30 days. It's not easy, but it's worth it, and I'm proud to say that I'm doing my part to reshape the leadership of Corporate America one person at a time.

One Company Doesn't Define Your Worth

It's tempting to let our self-worth be determined by a single employer or position when it comes to our careers. We place so much value on professional success that we neglect our intrinsic value.

People often introduce themselves by their occupation, such as "I am a lawyer" or "I work at Google," as if their jobs were the sum and substance of who they are. Recognizing our achievements is fine, but we shouldn't let that become our only identity.

Putting too much stock in our employment or the success of the business we work for can leave us exposed. It's common to experience a sense of personal loss when we lose our job, or our business goes bankrupt. Our self-esteem plummets when we don't believe in ourselves or our talents.

The reality is that neither our employer nor our job title has any bearing on our value as people. Each of us has value because of our own special blend of knowledge, experiences, and principles. Our value stems from the connections we make, the art we produce, and the changes we bring about in the world.

There is, of course, no doubting the significance of our jobs to our existence. Our careers give us security in our financial situations, meaning in our lives, and room to develop both personally and professionally. But we can't let those things be all that we are.

Putting too much stock in one's employment can be stifling. We risk missing other chances to learn and improve ourselves. There's also a risk that we won't give other interests outside work an opportunity to enrich our lives.

Instead, we should make it a priority to see our work not as the total of who we are but as one facet among many. While it's important to put in the effort required to reach our professional goals, it's also important to remember that life is about more than work.

It's up to us to determine where we place our value. We shouldn't let an employer determine our value. Instead, we should establish it for ourselves.

Starting Over is Scary After the Age of 40

Many people view turning 40 as a watershed moment in their lives. It's an opportunity to take stock of their progress and set new goals for the future. Many people experience anxiety and doubt during this period, particularly when making major life adjustments. It takes a lot of bravery and resolve to start over after age 40, so it's no wonder that many people give up on the idea.

Fear of the unexpected is a significant barrier to a fresh start after age 40. It's common for people to feel like they can't progress toward their goals because they've become too content with the status quo. It can be scary to consider uprooting your life and starting fresh after so long in the same place. Anxiety and reluctance can arise from the fear of failing. It can also come from uncertainty and having to start from nothing.

The pressure to succeed is another major challenge. Many people have multiple financial commitments by the time they hit 40. These include a mortgage, the cost of their children's schooling, and even a retirement fund. The pressure to make rapid progress toward financial stability and security can amplify the stress of starting over. Couple that with the previously mentioned variables and imagine the stress levels.

Moreover, ageism is a genuine problem in modern culture. Older people may find it difficult to land new jobs or be regarded seriously as business owners due to age-based biases. Potential employers and investors may view older people as less active. This makes it difficult and frustrating for them to show their worth.

Despite these drawbacks, beginning again after age 40 has many advantages. It's a chance to focus on what you've always wanted to do but had to put it on the back burner because of your obligations. It's an opportunity to broaden your horizons, test your mettle, and build something better for yourself. Beginning again with all the information and wisdom you've acquired over the years can be a great advantage. It will help guide your decision-making and problem-solving.

It's important to figure out what you want to achieve in your personal life, work life, and finances at any age. Then work backwards from those goals to create a plan to reach them successfully.

A Quote from the Movie "Point Break"

"Fear causes hesitation, and hesitation will cause your worst fears to come true. If you want the ultimate, you've got to be willing to pay the ultimate price."

Bodhi, Point Break

The words spoken by Bodhi in "Point Break" ring true. Fear can easily overcome us and prevent us from taking the steps necessary to realize our goals. Even worse, the more we think and procrastinate, the more likely it is that our worst worries will come true. We trap ourselves in a cycle from which we cannot escape.

But there is an escape plan. To overcome our anxieties, we must confront them head-on. Irrespective of our fears, now is the time to pursue our dreams and goals. It won't be simple and may require us to leave our comfort zones, but it's worth it if it means finally having the existence we've always dreamed of. We can overcome our fears and live our finest lives if we dare to do so.

Overcome Fear with This Formula

Here's a classic formula to overcome your fear. It's nothing that you aren't aware of.

It's quite straightforward:

1. Get the support you need for success (coaches, mentors etc.)
2. Keep promises to yourself

Getting much-needed help to conquer our fears is the first move toward achieving our goals. There are many people in our lives who can assist in this capacity including coaches, mentors, companions, and family members. It's important to have a support system in place to help us overcome feelings of isolation. That way we can move forward with our goals despite our apprehensions.

Finding people who have done what we want to do and asking for their help can give a huge boost. These people can shed light on the situation, tell us about their experiences, and point us in the right direction.

Keeping our word to ourselves is the second part of the formula for overcoming dread. Setting attainable goals, creating a strategy, and keeping promises are all part of this. Making and keeping personal commitments strengthens self-confidence and self-esteem. Both are crucial for conquering fear.

The odds of us achieving our goals improve when we break them down into smaller, more manageable tasks. We should also celebrate each small victory along the road because it will help us remain motivated and keep moving forward.

Famously, the Marines are known for teaching all members to make their beds every morning. This is a poignant metaphor for how personal growth is the first step toward making a difference in the world. Every morning, we must begin by preparing our bed. Though seemingly unimportant, this ritual helps us kick off each day with self-discipline and a feeling of having accomplished something.

Making the bed is a simple way to set the tone for a productive day and feel more in charge of your life. Over time, these small victories add up. They can give us the conviction and resolve to take on larger obstacles.

Additionally, when we make positive changes to ourselves, we motivate those around us to do the same. Being a positive role model increases the likelihood that others will adopt similar practices because actions speak louder than words. Changing the world is a lengthy process, but we can begin by changing ourselves.

<u>Takeaway</u>

- Fear is a major roadblock for people considering starting their businesses. Common worries include losing money, messing up, and failing.
- To help accomplish goals, fear can be converted into action.
- Never forget the value of doing your own thing, controlling what you can, and discovering your unique path to making a substantial difference in the world.
- Being honest, standing firm in one's beliefs, and making choices are all crucially important.
- Improve the lives of others, whether through global transformation or neighborhood improvement.

Chapter 7

Life by Design

"We all have two choices: we can make a living, or we can design a life."

Jim Rohn

In the movie "Groundhog Day," Bill Murray plays a TV weatherman who is trapped in a time loop. He must keep repeating the same day over and over again.

This may sound like a silly premise, but many people experience something similar in real life. They go through life without thinking about what they're doing.

Every day is the same:

- Get up

- get some coffee
- take the kids to school
- drive to work
- sit through the same meetings we sit through every week
- come home
- make dinner
- tuck the kids in
- watch TV until we're too tired to move

Sound familiar? It's not just you. Many of us seem to be stuck in a never-ending cycle of doing the same activities repeatedly. Perhaps you've been so busy with this routine that you feel like you're going in circles. Perhaps you've told yourself that you'll finally be able to make some changes when the kids move out, when you land that dream job, or when you launch your own company.

The question is, though, why put off today for tomorrow? Why put off living the great life you were meant to live? Skip the waiting room and start living your life on your own terms today. It's as simple as adopting a new perspective, being receptive to innovative ideas, and giving them a shot.

Life By Design

Living a life by design means coexisting with everything that holds meaning for you. It's about designing your life around your passions, even if it requires a lot of demanding work to get there.

A life by design allows you to be true to who you are. To me, that's what it's all about - being true to yourself and living your truth. I believe that living transparently and honestly is our responsibility, and this process starts with speaking the truth. Honest living isn't just a core value; it's a fundamental aspect of living a fulfilling life.

Identify Your Core Values and Goals

Having a solid sense of direction and purpose is crucial when designing your life. This is why it's so important to identify your fundamental values and goals. Your goals are the concrete outcomes you hope to accomplish in various areas of your life. Your fundamental values are the beliefs and principles that underpin everything you do. It's helpful to have a clear picture of your highest priorities when making purposeful decisions. This allows you to focus your efforts where they will have the most significant impact.

Finding your core values and goals can help you live life by your real priorities. People are too busy dealing with the mundane tasks of daily life - such as jobs, family, and other commitments - to stop and think about what they value most. When you know what you value highest, you can act in a manner that reflects those ideals. Setting specific goals can also help you stay on track with your goals. It keeps you from getting sidetracked by unimportant distractions.

Finding your core values and goals can also boost your happiness and feelings of accomplishment. Few people feel pleased or satisfied when they don't know where they're going or what they're working toward, even if they stumble into money and fame.

Knowing what you value most and working toward those goals can help you make tough decisions. When deciding between two alternatives, thinking about how each relates to your values and goals helps you feel less anxious and affords greater clarity about your decisions.

When you have a clear idea of your values and goals, you can devote your time and resources more wisely. This can help you make decisions more easily, improve feelings of fulfillment and happiness, and align your life with your true priorities.

Identify the People You Will Work With

The people you work with at an organization are an integral part of your success. Ensure both your values and their values are congruent with those of the business - and not just because you want to get along with your coworkers.

When a team shares ideals, everyone experiences a sense of purpose and contribution to the success of the organization. When an individual's values and those of the company line up, their job has meaning and significance. This can boost output, inspiration, and contentment in work.

On the other hand, when someone's beliefs differ from their organization's goals, results include a lack of motivation, conflict, and frustration. A lack of harmony between an organization's values and those of its workers can hurt the whole team.

In general, it's helpful to know who you'll be working with at a new job. That can shed light on whether the company culture is a good match for you.

The values, purpose, and goals of an organization all contribute to company culture. So do management style, the office atmosphere, and interactions between employees. When people feel like they belong at work, they are more productive, and the atmosphere is more uplifting.

Not everyone will find a company whose values are compatible with their own, and that's okay if you're just trying to make a paycheck. But working for a business whose values align with yours can impact your happiness at work and quality of life. Remember that your beliefs may evolve. It's fine to reevaluate the degree to which your company's tenets reflect your own. If they no longer align, it may be time to part ways.

Becoming Obsessed with Life by Design

When I started aiming to design my life on purpose, I investigated things like making vision boards, manifesting, and praying. To my surprise, my vision boards became increasingly effective. For example, I created a vision board for the first quarter of this year, and on January 1st, I had already achieved everything on it. This kind of success used to take me years to achieve. There's momentum that builds when you have a clear focus and vision for what you want to create in your life.

I can only think of one organization that truly embodies this mindset, and that's Gary Vee's VaynerMedia. Gary has a top-level employee called the Chief Heart Officer, who is in charge of understanding what motivates the company's staff. He understands that people are the key to a successful business, not the other way around.

"People move businesses, businesses don't move people."

Brandon Dawson

Vision Boards

Create a vision board if you need help figuring out how to get started on the path that will lead you to your goals and dreams. A vision board is a tool for visualizing your goals, dreams, and desires to help you achieve them. There is, however, a caveat. You must follow through. Creating a vision board can be a lot of fun and can help you plan a more wholesome lifestyle, but it's pointless if you don't act.

Happy Board = Vision Board

I prefer to refer to my vision board as a "bliss board" or "happiness board" because looking at it should make you happy.

Think about the answers to the following questions as you create your vision board:

- Does it make you happy?
- How do you achieve your goals and dreams?

Make your home and life exactly what you've always dreamed of with the help of your "happiness board." Make a strategy for each picture that specifies the actions needed to reach the destination. Share your hopes and dreams for the future with your spouse. Create a family vision board and ask for guidance as you put your plans into action.

When major changes occur in your life, whether planned or unplanned, you must readjust. The vision board won't become "wrong," but it may need revision as circumstances change. These boards can record how your desires and values evolve. As you learn more about who you are and how God has uniquely designed you to fulfill your mission in this world, your vision board will evolve.

You see, God can work and move things in our favor, but only when we allow our hearts and desires to shape reality. The following quote is one of my favorites. It accurately captures the feeling of having divine intervention and support for deepest wishes.

"And, when you want something, all the universe conspires in helping you to achieve it."

Paulo Coelho, The Alchemist

Jordan Peterson – Building the Day You Want

Peterson frequently discusses the idea of "building the day you want" in his speeches. This concept refers to choosing how to spend each day and working toward that goal. Peterson thinks it's essential for people to know what they want out of life, then make consistent efforts to achieve those goals.

One of Peterson's suggestions for creating the kind of day you want is to figure out what really matters to you. Then base your daily decisions on those values. He also stresses the significance of goal-setting and constant progress toward those goals (Peterson, 2018).

Peterson encourages his disciples to take baby steps toward the life they envision. For instance, make your bed and straighten up your room first thing in the morning, as he recommends. Doing even a few of these things can help you feel more accomplished and give you more energy for the rest of the day.

Success Isn't Linear

The path to success isn't a straight line. It's a long road with plenty of curves, bumps, and detours along the way. It certainly doesn't happen quickly either.

Being too hard on yourself in pursuit of success is a common pitfall. But dread is the brother of perfectionism. It can be so overwhelming that we freeze up and refuse to try anything new. Doubt is a significant contributor to insecurity, worry, and even clinical melancholy. The ability to admit fault, gain insight from it, and move on is much more valuable.

One reason many people quit too soon is that they imagine the path to success to be smooth sailing. However, this is not even close to being accurate. At times, you may experience difficulties or obstacles. It's especially important to maintain focus and drive during these moments. While pausing to evaluate our progress is healthy, we must always remember the importance of getting back up and continuing to make progress.

<u>Takeaway</u>

- You can indeed design the life you want. All it takes is some willpower and a mindset shift.
- Nothing is impossible and you can have what you dream of.
- Identify your core values and goals.
- Identify the people you are going to work with.
- Create vision boards.
- Build the day you want.
- Success isn't linear.

Chapter 8

Guilt and Shame Are Optional

"Guilt is always hungry, don't let it consume you."

Terri Guillemets

When was the last time you felt remorse for your actions? Maybe it was for something as simple as eating an entire pizza by yourself or as serious as making an error at work or saying something hurtful to a loved one. Whatever the cause, regret has the potential to paralyze us and prevent us from functioning normally.

But what if I told you that feelings of guilt and humiliation aren't mandatory? What if we could overcome the burden of guilt and humiliation by admitting our faults, gaining wisdom from them, and moving on with our lives?

In this chapter, we'll talk about how you can choose whether to feel bad about yourself. We'll talk about the harm caused by these feelings and suggest ways to change our perspective to be kinder and more merciful to ourselves. Let's get rid of our heavy burden of regret and humiliation so we can enjoy life more freely.

Let me share some important things I've learned from a trauma counsel. First and most importantly, negative emotions can be healed, even in the middle of extreme distress.

The effects of trauma, in whatever shape it takes, can be devastating. Emotions like guilt and dread are challenging to let go of, but I've found that acknowledging and processing them can help. It's not a picnic, but we can achieve a more tranquil and optimistic outlook with time and effort.

I can attest personally to the healing power of adventure travel for trauma survivors. To change our mentality and perspective, we need to step outside our usual routines and familiar environments.

Self-Inflicted Wounds

It's common to feel bad about ourselves when we compare ourselves to others or set an impossible benchmark for ourselves. Sometimes we fail to meet the standards of ourselves or others, and this can leave us feeling like a failure.

The problem is that these feelings are rarely grounded in fact. No human being is flawless. When we don't embrace our shortcomings and learn from them, but instead punish ourselves for them, we hold ourselves back.

Shame is another self-inflicted wound. There are times when we feel guilty about something that occurred to us or something we did, even if it wasn't our fault. The acts of others or external factors may leave us feeling like it's our fault.

When we feel guilty or ashamed, it's because we're punishing ourselves. These are emotions that we've cultivated on the inside and must learn to release.

To overcome feelings of remorse and shame, the first step is realizing that your feelings are hurting you only because you let them. We're the ones afflicting ourselves with these feelings, and we can set them free at any time.

The next step is to treat ourselves with more compassion. We need to recognize that our flaws are natural. When we err, we should treat ourselves kindly and try to improve rather than beat ourselves up.

Finally, pay greater attention to the here and now. We can't alter what's already happened. We have no say over what will happen in the future. However, we have complete power over our thoughts and actions right now.

A Personal Guilt

Becoming a mother has brought me the strongest feeling of guilt I've ever experienced. You may have heard of "mom guilt." It happens when we worry that we aren't being responsible or following societal expectations. However, I eventually realized that the main cause of my guilt was the negative thoughts and beliefs I had about my abilities as a mother. It was tough to accept, but I needed to let go of my feelings of regret if I wanted to move on.

I recognized these same feelings of guilt in many of the CEOs I've worked with. Many of them carry the burden of regret. They think they could have done something differently or should have made another choice. They think they would have been better off if they had taken another path. This mindset can make them feel like they have no control over their lives and like they're wandering without a purpose. It can also trap them in the past and prevent them from acting and living in the present moment. It's odd to talk to people who base their professional identities on things that happened years ago in their workplaces.

People have a habit, in my observation, of passing judgment on themselves based on memories and feelings of guilt and humiliation. The stress of dealing with financial problems and the emotional turmoil it causes can be devastating for those people. Eventually, they reach a point where they can't bear to make eye contact with their loved ones. In my role as a coach, I hear many people say that they wish they could just let go of their guilt and humiliation, but they don't know how.

I believe that if someone is open to forgiving themselves or changing the way they think, then they can stop feeling guilty or ashamed. Rather than becoming mired in an overly complicated process of letting go, we have the option of reframing the situation and moving on. We must check in with ourselves and see if we're in a place to rethink and let go.

Reframe Thoughts to Release Guilt

Guilt is a heavy burden that can crush our spirits and prevent us from living life to the fullest. It can keep us from appreciating the beauty and wonder of the here and now. The good news is that we can escape the prison of remorse by changing the way we look at things.

When we reframe our thinking, we replace a pessimistic and self-critical outlook with an optimistic and forgiving one. This process necessitates that we question the justifications we give for our actions, then seek out alternative, more helpful narratives.

Reframe negative thoughts like *"I'm an awful person for making that mess"* to more positive ones like *"I made a bad choice, but I can learn from it and do better next time."* Through this reframing, we can change our perspective and move on from the negative experience. The crippling effects of guilt are lessened as a result. Reclaim the power of confidence and self-compassion by shifting the focus from blame to development.

When we reframe our thinking, we aren't refusing to acknowledge any pain we may have caused to ourselves or others. Instead, we're admitting we messed up and accepting that human fallibility is a part of life.

This way, we can:

- acknowledge our mistakes,
- make amends if required, and
- move on with the confidence that comes from knowing we have room to develop and improve.

Simply put, changing the way we look at things can help us let go of regret to embrace a more optimistic and productive outlook on life. It's not always simple, and it might take some time and effort to perfect, but knowing how to process and let go of guilt is an invaluable skill. If you feel guilt creeping up on you, consider pausing and reevaluating your situation. This simple self-check-in has the potential to alter your outlook and your existence in profound ways.

The Rat Park Study

In the 1970s, psychologist Bruce Alexander performed the Rat Park study. It showed that rats subjected to a stimulating and social environment were less likely to become addicted to cocaine compared to those subjected to isolation and barren cages (Sederer, 2020). The research ran counter to the prevalent view at the time that addiction was the fault of individuals or the drugs themselves, with no consideration for the environmental and social factors at play.

In the experiment, rats were housed in either tiny, individual cages or larger cages where they could interact with other rats and play with toys. While rats in both conditions had access to cocaine-laced water, those in the former were less apt to drink from it.

Alexander concluded that the substance itself is not the only cause of addiction. Rather, several factors including genetics, society, and the environment all play a role. He theorized that addiction is a product of an absence of connectedness and meaning in one's life. Therefore, he proposed that providing companionship, meaning, and a feeling of belonging could prevent or lessen addiction.

This study demonstrates how crucial cultural and environmental factors are. Contextual factors also play a role in shaping feelings of guilt and shame. Children subjected to harsh judgment and humiliation carry those feelings into adulthood. Symptoms of this can range from a lack of confidence to anxiety, sadness, and even substance abuse.

A lack of meaning or good social connections, like the rats in the research, may make people more vulnerable to guilt and shame. Those surrounded by positive influences and have a clear sense of direction in life may be better able to change their perspective and let go of negative emotions like remorse and shame.

Moreover, the study suggests that modifying surroundings can help fight against addiction. Similarly, a person's surroundings and societal setting can be changed to lessen their experience of guilt and shame. This may entail reaching out to trusted loved ones, visiting a therapist or counselor, or simply learning to be kinder and more forgiving to yourself.

Dealing with Guilt and Shame

Feelings of guilt and shame can have a devastating effect on our lives, particularly in the professional sphere. High-ranking leaders are often put under pressure to portray an air of authority and success. But when remorse and shame weigh us down, what happens? What impact do these feelings have on our ability to make decisions and our career's ultimate success?

In these high-pressure managerial roles, you simply cannot fake success. You can't expect to make it through trying circumstances by faking assurance. Work, interactions with coworkers and clients, and career progress will all suffer if you're harboring feelings of guilt and shame.

Guilt and Shame Clouds Your Decision-Making Power

Feelings of guilt and shame can cloud one's judgment and make it difficult to act sensibly. If you let negative feelings overwhelm you, you may end up making decisions that aren't beneficial to you or your business. You may second-guess your decisions or be afraid to take chances, both of which can prevent you from reaching your full potential.

Redefine Who You Are

Negative feelings can be conquered by reflecting on how you define yourself. Past failures don't define you, nor do the opinions of others or societal norms. What defines you is who you are right now and your capacity for growth and development.

Be Aware of Your Energy and Frequency

Taking stock of your vitality and frequency is an effective place to start the process of redefinition. How would you describe the energy you're sending out into the world? Do you have a lot of positive energy and self-confidence, or do negative thoughts and self-doubt weigh you down? The kind of opportunities you encounter in life is directly proportional to the frequency you radiate. Focusing on positive emotions and increasing your frequency can help you manifest the professional and personal success you seek.

Attract and Control the Career that You Want

A career transformation entails more than just switching employers or rising through the ranks. It's about making fundamental changes in every aspect of your existence. It requires an introspective examination of core beliefs and practices, then implementing deliberate adjustments to align them with one's ambitions.

Being courageous mandates facing fears and doing things that cause unease and uncertainty. Take charge of your professional destiny if you ever hope to land the job you want. This entails actively looking for ways to improve yourself and putting forth the effort necessary to achieve success. Rather than allowing feelings of guilt and shame to hold you back, accept responsibility for your actions and grow from them.

Empathy and Forgiveness

Developing empathy and forgiveness for oneself is the ultimate secret to letting go of professional guilt and shame. Accept that you are fallible and that blunders are an integral part of your education. Focus on what you've learned and how you've improved because of your mistakes rather than beating yourself up over them.

<u>Takeaway</u>

- You can overcome feelings of guilt and shame and find the success and satisfaction you've been seeking by taking responsibility for your life and work decisions.
- Redefine who you are.
- Become aware of your energy and frequency.
- Keep in mind that you are the master of your fate and that with effort, focus, and optimism, you can achieve anything you put your mind to.
- Guilt and shame cloud your judgment.
- Attract and control the career you want.
- Show yourself empathy and forgiveness.

Chapter 9

Delegation and Automation

"When something is important enough, you do it even if the odds are not in your favor."

Elon Musk

For many company owners, freedom and personal liberation are elusive ideals. It's common for people to feel boxed in by the routines of running a thriving business. Thanks to the boundless opportunities presented by technology, we can now automate processes, share responsibility, and work from afar while maintaining full control of our businesses.

As business owners and operators, we always seek methods to cut costs without sacrificing quality.

When you're trying to figure out what to do, it helps to ask yourself these two questions:

1. Why do I want to do this?
2. How can I make sure I don't have to do it again in the future?

Using this method, you can improve the efficiency of your business. How then can we break free from the bonds of boring and repetitive labor? The first step is to get clear of all the unnecessary stuff. How many tasks do we have to complete? Must you handle each one by yourself, or in the same way you always have?

Many of your current responsibilities could be taken on by others. However, before you get started, you should make sure they are necessary tasks. If you could streamline, automate, or delegate all but the most essential duties, imagine how much time it would save.

The idea that putting in more time at work will improve results is widespread yet flawed. When making a choice, prioritize efficacy over efficiency. You can't be effective at anything unless it moves you closer to your objectives. If you want to maximize your productivity at work, evaluate your

SWOT (strengths, weaknesses, chances, and threats) to focus on the most worthwhile tasks.

Hiring a Nanny — Delegation

The decision to hire a nanny was the best thing I could have done for my child and my company. Getting over my misgivings about entrusting others with my son's care was challenging, but it was well worth it. Two years into her time with us, our nanny has proven to be invaluable. The expense of childcare may be on the rise, but I've found that hiring a nanny frees me up to concentrate on my career and other interests. I get stress free time to spend feeling fully present with my son. I get to be a joyful mother! I've been able to get more done during the week because I also have a caterer come in twice a week to take care of the cooking.

To me, having money means having more independence, choices, and means of subsistence. I think it's critical, if finances permit it, to outsource routine chores to someone else. It is essential to reevaluate your career, financial, and personal objectives and reach out for help.

For women to get ahead in the professional world, they need to ignore the shame attached to seeking help with household chores. Hiring help has freed me from the burden of housework so that I can focus on my son and spend valuable time with him.

I firmly believe that putting your worth into "doing it all" as a badge of honor is a huge mistake. Having systems and processes in place and giving yourself the license to delegate tasks can free up your time and energy as a female CEO and mother.

Blue-Collar Mentality — Do Everything Yourself

"Blue-collar mentality" is a phrase that describes a certain outlook on life that values traits like hard work, self-reliance, effort, and perseverance. It's often associated with jobs that involve manual labor or are considered working-class, though it can be applied to any profession or pursuit.

Many people with this outlook adopt a "do-it-yourself" approach to life, refusing to ask for or accept assistance with anything. While such a mindset is often commended, particularly when it comes to work ethic and tenacity, it's not without its drawbacks. One downside is that a blue-collar mentality can make people reluctant to ask for help, even from those who have more experience or expertise than they do. This can make them less open to innovative ideas and experiences, which stunts personal development and progress.

That said, don't let others make every important choice. Exercise caution when taking counsel. We should be wary of taking advice from people who may not have lived the kind of existence we envision for ourselves. If they haven't had the same level of success or gained the same level of knowledge that we have, their advice may not be beneficial. There's no need to do everything yourself, but still, evaluate advice that comes from dubious sources.

Energy Is Finite – Use It Smartly

The "infinite number of tasks" that you have every day, every week, and every month won't go away no matter how hard you work (and I know some of you are trying). Stop working yourself to exhaustion and filling your day with less important tasks. The "need-to-do list" includes only the most crucial tasks that must be completed to succeed. Using the opportunity cost of each task, you can prioritize your "to-do" list items.

The term "opportunity cost" describes the potential gain that one foregoes in favor of an alternative decision. It's the value of the next best alternative that you give up when choosing one option over another. In other words, it's the "opportunity" you miss by doing something else. To make the most of your limited time and resources, prioritize tasks based on their opportunity cost. You can do this by creating a separate "need to do list" and ignoring everything else. By comparing the opportunity cost of each task to your "need-to-do list," you can decide which tasks are most essential.

You'll need to learn to confidently decline requests that don't directly contribute to meeting your goals. Even if your teammates can't complete an item on your "to-do" list as well as you can, practice assigning it to them anyway if it's not something that mandates your attention. By delegating tasks, you save time and concentrate on more important things. For example, by delegating notetaking at a meeting, you're free to focus on the main topics that need to be discussed.

Stop doing things that aren't essential just because you enjoy doing them; instead, focus on the tasks at hand. I'm aware of how frequently the boss tries to add items to your "to-do list." The trick to saying "no" without risk of getting fired is to draw their attention to the fact that their request will prevent you from accomplishing something else that's higher on your list of priorities.

Since they, too, are making decisions based on opportunity cost, most managers will realize it's more efficient to hire someone else to do menial tasks. Your time and stamina are limited, so make the most of them while you have them.

There's a concept in Japan called "Karoshi," or overwork mortality. It's exceedingly common there, as Japanese work culture pushes employees to work to their breaking point. Avoid overwork mortality by focusing on what's important.

Pay Attention to People's Passions When Delegating

When looking for someone to assist you, it's essential to consider their interests. This way, you can give them work that plays to their skillsets. This not only makes them happier at work but also keeps them from getting burned out.

If you give someone a job that they're genuinely interested in, they'll work harder and be happier with the results. If you force someone into a task they have no interest in, they may lose interest and eventually become unproductive.

Therefore, it's essential to look after the people you delegate tasks to by assigning them duties that match their interests and expertise. In addition to improving their performance, this will make them happier and more effective team members.

As a working woman, I often found it difficult to meet the demands of my home life and work life. I was struggling to take care of my child alone and was hesitant to ask for assistance. When I finally found a babysitter who was not only qualified but also enthusiastic about childcare, things began to look up.

My nanny has proven to be invaluable, even in areas outside of childcare. She had a flair for the culinary arts and an eye for interior design. She took pleasure in tidying up and cleaning, and she was always ready to lend a hand. Knowing her better led me to realize that her joy and contentment in her work originated from her abilities and interests.

Since these tasks interested her, I started giving her more responsibility in the kitchen and bathroom. She thrived in those roles, and she was always ready to take on new ones. I told her how appreciative I was of her efforts, and we discussed her professional ambitions. I found out that she wanted to train for a career as a PA, so I offered my assistance.

I've elevated her to the role of housekeeper because she does so much for me. She takes care of everything, from my calendar to my clothes. This is a win-win situation, since she now earns $80,000 annually, which is double what she earned before.

Recognizing my nanny's interests and abilities enabled me to give her more responsibility, freeing up my time for work and family. And as a result, she was able to develop professionally and do work she enjoyed. It worked out perfectly, and I'm incredibly pleased with the result.

Technological Automation

Keeping up with the never-ending list of tasks in today's work world is no easy feat. There's always something that needs doing whether it's handling administrative duties or monitoring social media profiles. That's why it's so important for entrepreneurs to have access to automation and delegation tools.

LinkedIn is a good example of a place where automation could prove helpful. Streamlining your LinkedIn outreach can save you time and energy. That can be done using automation tools and platforms. We have our automation tool for LinkedIn.

Here's the link to it:

https://esferas.io/

By utilizing our top-tier LinkedIn automation tool, you will be able to expand and speed up the growth of your network.

Freelance websites like Upwork and Fiverr are another option for assigning work. These platforms make it easy to connect with skilled individuals who can take on a variety of projects, from graphic design and content production to administrative duties. If you delegate, you'll have more time to concentrate on expanding your business.

Automating and delegating tasks can also be accomplished with the help of Google Docs, Excel Sheets, and Google Drive. These services allow the whole team to work together on projects and exchange files in real-time. They can help you remain on top of your game by keeping track of your to-dos, due dates, and project developments.

Finally, remember that popularity metrics like likes and comments aren't the be-all and end-all. Prioritize helping others and converting likes into business prospects instead. To expand your customer base and attract new customers, produce high-quality material. Also, maintain meaningful connections with your audience and respond to their feedback.

Takeaway

- Implementing automation and delegation increases productivity.
- Focus on your strengths while technology and contractors handle the rest of the work.
- Now is the time to begin investigating options for developing your company.

Chapter 10

Advocate for Yourself

"You, more than anyone or anything else are the cause for most of your suffering. Only when you understand this will you be able to change this?"

Akiroq Brost

The term "self-advocacy" is familiar to most people, but a clear definition never hurts. Self-advocacy boils down to being able to articulate your own needs. Self-advocates have a higher chance of succeeding in all aspects of life, in part because they are self-assured in their abilities.

Advocating for oneself is a path to autonomy. It gives people the ability to figure out ways to fix issues that other people haven't noticed.

There are three main components of self-advocacy:

1. Knowing what you require
2. Finding out what kind of assistance could be useful
3. Sharing your requirements with those around you

Let's look at a basic example. Imagine you're a student who has trouble with writing, perhaps because of a health condition. You're taking a history lesson, so you'll need to take plenty of notes.

If you're an advocate for yourself, you know that assistance, such as prewritten notes, can be useful. You go to your instructor and explain the situation, then request some handouts be made in advance. If your instructor says no, you can always talk to a guidance counselor or the department in charge of disability services.

On the other hand, if you aren't able to advocate for yourself, an inability to take notes becomes a major issue. You'll have a much more challenging time keeping up with each lesson, which sabotages your academic career. This is why self-advocacy is so important.

Weight Loss — A Personal Experience

I had a major epiphany about a year ago. I decided to prioritize my health and fitness, and after several months of effort, I improved my health. My frame of mind flourished, and I was pleased with the developments I had accomplished.

However, I soon discovered that no one cared about my new appearance, and no one was going to do the work for me. While I had plenty of supporters, this was my adventure. I had gambled on my abilities and won.

I invested in Cardone Ventures around that time intending to help it expand and reach new heights. But it seemed like no one was paying attention and it was up to me to make things happen. Once again, I had to put my faith in myself.

Therefore, it became crucial for me to focus on improving my outlook, self-assurance, and ability to advocate for myself. I knew no one would come to my aid, so I took it upon myself to defend my interests and those of my company. I had to tell myself I could do it and keep going.

It's easy to get caught up in trying to win the approval of those around you, but in the end, the only approval that counts is what you give yourself. We must take a chance on ourselves, improve our mindset, and advocate for ourselves to reach our objectives. If you find yourself in a rut or wondering if anyone cares, keep in mind that you are your strongest ally.

Keep going, trust yourself, and put your money where your mouth is. Even if the road ahead is rocky, if you keep your head down and keep plugging away, you can accomplish anything.

7 Advantages of Self-Advocacy

Self-advocacy is a crucial ability to master, and not just for professional success.

There are many positive outcomes from honing your ability to advocate for yourself and others:

1. Self-advocacy is a talent that can help you and those around you achieve your goals. By doing so, you create a place where people feel comfortable expressing themselves and succeeding.
2. You decide to steer your ship. You set limits and make value-driven decisions. You have a firm grasp of your values and the reasons behind them.
3. You gain confidence in your judgment as you learn more about yourself, other people, and the rules by which society operates.
4. When you talk to people, you ask them questions that let them talk at length. Your ability to understand and appreciate others' points of view grows.

5. You develop into a capable problem-solver. You can investigate the issue at hand and consider different viewpoints. You know that to achieve your goals, you must first offer a solution that is both logical and convincing.

6. You're always committed to self-improvement, and you're involved in groups that shape laws that affect you and the people around you.

7. Both you and those around you have a voice. Everyone benefits.

Keys to Advocate for Yourself

Advocating for yourself is especially important in the ever-changing world of corporate America. All the things I've outlined in this book must be in place before you can be in a position of power and effectively pivot. Next, we'll go over how to speak up for yourself and your company, as well as the value of never forgetting to adapt.

No One Is Coming to Save You

Realizing that no one will rescue you is the first step in learning to advocate for yourself. Your job and health depend on you taking charge of them and making your needs known when appropriate.

The Dopamine Illusion

The dopamine illusion occurs when we act based on a temporary rush of dopamine. This is a common pitfall when searching for new employment. For instance, after sending out one hundred resumes, you might feel successful regardless of whether any of them result in an offer. This is counterproductive and may cause unhappiness and resentment.

Instead, it's essential to utilize practices such as setting goals, making plans, building relationships, and practicing lifelong learning. These will get you farther than relying on fleeting emotions for motivation.

Get Out of Your Comfort Zone

The next move is to challenge your established habits and routines. It's simple to fall into a routine of putting off your responsibilities until tomorrow. However, you may need to leave your safe space if you want to expand your horizons and develop your skills. Expanding your horizons in the workplace, knowledge base, or social group can help you accomplish this goal.

Feel Armored Up Enough to Get Through Your Day

Having the confidence you need to get through the day is also important when standing up for yourself. Even if you must start small, commit to a set of positive, productive daily habits. Some examples of this would be exercising before work, meditating for five minutes first thing in the morning, or getting dressed for success. You'll feel more assured and capable as you go about your day thanks to these practices.

Be a champion for the company you work for. Being an active and contributing team member includes speaking up when you notice an issue or an area that could use improvement and suggesting potential solutions. Your work should reflect the values and priorities of the business, so know these values like the back of your hand.

When speaking up for yourself or your company, it's important to always keep changes in mind. The world is constantly shifting, so we must be flexible and open to new experiences. Be receptive to novelty, willing to experiment, and open to using innovative tools. By anticipating changes before they happen, we can set ourselves and our companies up for long-term success.

Takeaway

- To design your life, advocate for yourself and your company. This means taking charge of your job and health, getting out of your comfort zone, making good daily habits, and always getting better at what you know and how you do things.

- It's important to be aggressive and interested in your work and to make sure that your goals match those of the company.
- Don't forget about growth.
- Be ready to change and adapt to the world around you.
- Make your life what you want it to be.

Chapter 11

Belief Lids

"If you don't give education to people, it is easy to manipulate them."

Pele

How often do you feel like your opinions are suppressed by the norms of society? You might feel that you can't have lofty goals or follow your heart because they don't correspond to society's preconceived notions of success. If so, you're not alone.

While the concept of limiting beliefs is not new to me, the phrase "belief lids" only recently came to my attention after I began working with Cardone Ventures. There are, as I have emphasized throughout this work, multiple layers to this journey. When I put my advice into practice and keep my eye on the prize, my degree of success increases, and I can accomplish even more. This lets the lid off my beliefs, and from there, I can set fresh goals and tackle my doubts one by one.

It's helpful to hang out with others who are succeeding in their endeavors and who have had the kind of life events that have changed their perspectives. Spending time with these kinds of people gives you a broader worldview. But in the managerial realm, it often takes much more time to blow a belief lid off. This was hard for me to accept because, as entrepreneurs, we tend to set lofty goals for ourselves and surround ourselves with others who do the same. The question, "Where am I going?" occupies our minds constantly.

The clients I work with should have the same outlook, but they often suffer from limiting beliefs that sabotage their success. The realization of your goal and the realization of your vision board are not the same things, and there is no final destination. You simply advance to the next tier and, ideally, a higher standard of living.

Many people can go their whole lives without noticing that they've been underestimating themselves. They think they've plateaued, but don't realize there's always something more challenging to accomplish.

The spiritual high of overcoming rigid beliefs is intoxicating. You'll feel compelled to keep going as soon as you lift one of these limiting assumptions. Making this foundational change benefits everyone involved: you, your loved ones, your neighborhood, your company, and the world.

Each of us has a "belief lid" that prevents us from reaching our full potential. These ideas about ourselves, usually shaped by social norms, prevent us from acting on our deepest desires. You might think you aren't qualified for a certain field or that you're too old to acquire a new skill. The reality, however, is that there is always more to learn. If we are willing to break through our self-imposed belief lids, we can accomplish anything. The first step is realizing you hold these limited ideas and making a conscious effort to overcome them.

Love and encouragement from my spouse Tim were crucial to my success in removing my belief lids. He encouraged me to follow my goals even when I lacked faith in them myself. He urged me to keep challenging myself further than I had before, saying that I could always improve.

Those who sense the constraints of their own belief lids should realize they are not alone. It's time to discard those stifling assumptions and conformist ideas. Have faith in yourself and realize that there is always more to achieve. If you're lucky enough to have someone believe in you as much as Tim has, cherish that person. With Tim's unflinching faith in me, I know that if we work together, we can make our goals come true and create the life we've always imagined for ourselves.

<u>Takeaway</u>

- Formed typically by societal standards and self-limiting beliefs, our "belief lids" are the limiting factors that keep us from realizing our complete potential. However, if we can overcome these restrictions, we can accomplish anything we set our minds to. Recognizing the existence of such self-defeating ideas and actively working to change them is the first step.
- It's crucial to surround yourself with positive, supportive people and to set increasingly tricky goals for yourself if you hope to develop personally and professionally.
- We can make our dreams come true if we stick together and have faith in ourselves.

Conclusion

I'm filled with anticipation and confidence as I turn the final page of this book. Writing this book has been an adventure that's led me into the depths of my psyche to face the obstacles that were once in my way, and I hope reading it has had a similar effect. Confronting these obstacles has also shown us that the very same fear that held us back in the past can be converted into a source of motivation and success.

Fear is not something to be ashamed of or avoided; this much we have learned from the experiences of those who have conquered their own fears and the advice of professionals in the field. It's a component of being human, and when welcomed, it can help us grow in ways we never imagined. It's not a lack of fear that enables people to go on to achieve remarkable things; rather, those who are able to channel their fears into positive action achieve success.

We've covered everything from imposter syndrome to the fear of failing, and we've come away from this book with the knowledge that any of these fears can be conquered with the right approach and collection of resources. We have learned that the first step toward conquering our phobias is to gain a more profound knowledge of ourselves and our fears.

We can overcome our fears in several ways, including through meditation, counseling, and open communication with others.

The most valuable takeaway from this book, though, is that success is about more than just arriving at our destination. The most rewarding jobs are not the ones that come easily but the ones that require us to work hard, be persistent, and confront our fears head-on. The most successful people are often those who have failed the most, and this is a lesson we have learned: failure is not something to be dreaded but rather a chance to learn and develop.

Now that we've reached the end of the book, I pray that you've been encouraged to face your fears and go after the job of your desires. No matter where you are in your professional life, there is always space for development and progress. Using your fears as motivation, you can accomplish goals you never imagined possible and design a life you love.

Thank you for coming along on this adventure with me and for facing your own personal challenges head-on. I hope that you have found this book to be a helpful guide and that you will keep the advice and strategies you've learned there as fuel for your own success. Remember that your only real obstacle is the fear that prevents you from reaching your full potential. Get out there, confront your demons, and live the life of your desires. The universe is ready for you!

Made in United States
Troutdale, OR
10/15/2023

13726347R00077